Rush Limbaugh and the Bible

Rush Limbaugh and the Bible

Daniel J. Evearitt

HORIZON HOUSE PUBLISHERS
CAMP HILL, PENNSYLVANIA

Horizon House Publishers
3825 Hartzdale Drive, Camp Hill, PA 17011

ISBN: 0–88965–104–3
LOC Catalog Card Number: 93–61103
© 1993 by Horizon House Publishers
All rights reserved
Printed in the United States of America

93 94 95 96 97 5 4 3 2 1

Subject Photos: John Livzey/Dot
Bibles Photo: Carl S. Socolow

Dedication

This book is dedicated to my brother
Terry,
a confirmed "dittohead."

Endnote Abbreviations

RL	=	Rush Limbaugh, *The Way Things Ought To Be*
RLRS	=	The Rush Limbaugh Radio Show
LL	=	The Limbaugh Letter
RLTS	=	The Rush Limbaugh Television Show

Contents

Publisher's Preface

Mandating a book like this has been an interesting process. It may have begun in my car when I found myself listening in bemused amazement to Rush. Was I about to become a some-kind-of-a-percentage "dittohead"? I also began to notice the parallels (and divergences) between the radio shows and the Bible.

Next, I was working on another manuscript of an upcoming title by Dan Evearitt. I liked the writing. And I sensed that Dan's skill and background applied to the Rush Limbaugh phenomenon might certainly result in a helpful book.

After Dan agreed to take on the project, there were the necessary delimitations. We were obviously not interested in an exposé of anything. Since the book was to be focused on ideas, it could not be exhaustive in any sense, nor was it intended to be. But it will become part of the Limbaugh literature.

Our motive has been to play a part in the ongoing attempt by millions of listeners to "get a handle" on Rush. Welcome to the process.

K. Neill Foster
Executive Vice President/Publisher

Introduction

*E*valuating a moving target can be a bit hard to do. Rush Limbaugh comes on with the force of what seems at times like a hurricane. He attempts to blast aside all the arguments in his way. He does not lend himself well to a still life portrait. Trying to come to grips with his basic message involved examining radio broadcasts, television shows, his writings and articles written about him.

Every attempt has been made to accurately reflect his statements on the issues discussed. A request for an interview made through his chief of staff, Kit Carson, was respectfully turned down. Mr. Limbaugh did not want to be quoted chapter and verse on issues related to the Bible.

In addition to the Rush Limbaugh radio and television shows, his book, *The Way Things Ought To Be*, provided food for thought. Material gathered from back issues of *The Limbaugh Letter*, graciously supplied by its managing editor, Diana Schneider, also helped me gain a perspective on the Limbaugh message.

My profound appreciation for the patience of my wife throughout the time spent on this project must not go unmentioned.

What you have before you is an examination of Rush Limbaugh from a biblical, evangelical Christian perspective. This phenomenally successful communicator means various things to various people. Hopefully this book will help you to gain a biblical perspective on Rush Limbaugh's manner and message.

Daniel J. Evearitt

Detroit Free Press columnist Bob Talbert writes, "I hate many of Rush Limbaugh's antiquated and archaic attitudes, yet I love his show."

Limbaugh describes himself as an entertainer *first* and a conservative *second*.

John McCollister, *The Saturday Evening Post*

The show is devoted exclusively to what I think. I do not attempt to find out what the people of the country are thinking.

RL

This is no "harmless little fuzzball," as he would have us believe. Nor is he "the most dangerous man in America," as some of his ideological foes have argued.

The real Rush Limbaugh, controversial though he is, stands somewhere between those two poles. But far be it from them to call him a centrist. Front and center, yes. But centrist? Never.

Paul D. Colford, The Rush Limbaugh Story

A "Prophet"
with Honor

A hybrid prophet–comedian with an audience of millions does not exactly fit the prophetic mold.

The lonely prophet of old, feet dusty from the weary trail, life in danger because leaders and populace alike resent his bold, doomsday warnings, would be more appropriate.

But that image hardly fits the reigning prophet of political conservatism in America. Prophets of old were often without honor in their own countries. Such is certainly not the case with Rush Limbaugh. Not only do his radio and television audiences lavish praise upon him, but advertisers reward him with a handsome income.

Rush's Fame

On the air each weekday on over 600 U.S. radio stations in 1993, as well as on shortwave worldwide, Limbaugh reaches in excess of 20 million listeners per week. His daily television show, a half-hour video critique of current events has, within its first year, become the number three rated late-night show in the nation.

His first book, *The Way Things Ought To Be*, immediately went to the top of the *New York Times* nonfiction bestsellers list, where it stayed for months. It has been rated by both Waldenbooks and Barnes and Noble as their "bestselling hardcover nonfiction title of all time." *See, I Told You So*, his forthcoming second book, featuring more provocative commentary on social and political issues, promises to be equally as successful.[1]

Limbaugh's personal appearances, billed as "Rush to Excellence," sell out. He has even attracted hundreds of his fans who pay $1,500 to take seminar-filled ocean cruises with him. He has sponsored the National Conservative Forum, gatherings of conservative thinkers, writers and politicians for day-long speech-fests and discussions held before an audience.

He invites his national audience to study at

the mythical Limbaugh Institute for Advanced Conservative Studies. In reality, this is the free process of learning his brand of conservatism through faithful attention to his radio and television shows. He claims to hold the "Attila the Hun Chair" on its make-believe faculty.

In May, 1993, an enthusiastic supporter sponsored a bake sale in front of his Fort Collins, Colorado home to raise the $29.95 subscription price of the 300,000-circulation monthly *Limbaugh Letter*. Limbaugh got wind of it and parlayed it into a major happening. Some 75,000 people from all over the country attended this all-day media event. Speeches, music, entertainment and an appearance by Limbaugh himself made "Dan's Bake Sale," as it was billed, the largest bake sale in history.

When he advocated wearing a "Deficit Spending Awareness Ribbon" to show concern about the growing federal deficit, the folded dollar bill "ribbons" began showing up on people's lapels from coast to coast, even on Capitol Hill. The symbols not only made a statement, but, at the same time, they challenged the whole concept of wearing ribbons to show concern about an issue. Limbaugh finds those who wear colored ribbons to be sanctimonious snobs, trying to show that they care more than others.[2]

Limbaugh claims that over 300 restaurants nationwide have set aside "Rush Rooms" where patrons gather to listen to his radio show while they lunch.[3] Most of the diners, according to reports, are males. They gather to listen and cheer, much as at a sporting event, as Limbaugh scores points for conservatism against the liberal opposition.

Various items bearing Limbaugh's likeness and slogans are available. "Rush Is Right" bumper stickers and Rush T-shirts are popping up across the land.

Gaining Respect

At the same time, Limbaugh has been gaining a growing respect among some members of the political establishment in Washington. Conservative—and liberal—politicians consider him a force to be reckoned with.

Both President George Bush and Vice President Dan Quayle paid visits to Limbaugh's radio show during the 1992 election campaign. Limbaugh even spent an overnight in the White House, at Bush's invitation.

Former-President Ronald Reagan dropped him a note in December, 1992, which Limbaugh published in his newsletter. Reagan praised him as "the number one voice for conservatism in our country."[4]

Liberals begrudgingly are being forced to pay attention to him. He has become the leader of an invisible army of politically conservative Americans who are united through the airwaves. Although Limbaugh usually makes a point of not soliciting calls or letters to specific politicians, congresspersons or government officials, some might find their mailboxes overflowing in reaction to Limbaugh's passing comment made about them on radio or TV. When he has, on rare occasions, asked people to call the White House or Congress to register reaction to an issue, the phone circuits have overloaded.

Why all this fame and attention? Quite simply, Rush Limbaugh is funny. Those who agree with him of course find his humor more to their liking than do those who disagree. But even some liberals laugh, though they may feel a bit guilty about what they are laughing at.

Interspersed throughout his radio show are "Updates" on some of Limbaugh's pet concerns. Introduced by a theme song, these broadsides target environmentalists, animal rights activists, condom distribution advocates, feminists and others. Holding opposing views up to ridicule is the mainstay of Limbaugh's radio and television programs. In fact, the genius of his style is comedy. One has to listen closely to determine if Limbaugh is serious or just having some fun.

Does Limbaugh mind all the laughter? Not at all. He views himself as an entertainer. His goal is to build as large an audience as possible.[5] And he appears to be succeeding.

The Focus of His Shows

The focus of his call-in radio show is decidedly about *his* views, not the callers'. People tune in to hear *him*. His calls are screened to funnel attention to issues of interest. A dull caller is seen as death to ratings.[6] Calls are often little more than short remarks which launch Limbaugh on another monologue about an issue.

If one is looking for an unbiased, balanced overview of current events it will definitely not be found on either Limbaugh's radio or television show. His message is a counterattack on what he views to be the liberal bias of the "dominant media culture" in America. He often exaggerates to the point of distorting the views he opposes. He repeatedly claims that he need not give equal time to opposing views. The other side has the television networks, cable news outlets, news magazines and countless newspapers espousing the liberal slant on current events. He sees himself as the alternative. As he is fond of asserting, "I *am* equal time!"[7]

Rush Limbaugh is the most successful personality in the field of talk radio. He got there by being interesting. He is a comedian and a showman. Political commentary, while essential, is couched in humor. Even those who violently object to him find themselves tuning in to see how he will verbally skewer their cherished ideas.

Over the years there have been many other politically conservative talk show hosts on local radio stations. In an effort to please their core audience some of them deliberately enraged callers by rudely hanging up on those they disagreed with. Sometimes they would make offensive comments just to be outrageous and gain attention.

Limbaugh is different. He is usually polite on the phone. At times he will go to great lengths to let a caller express a viewpoint with which he has major problems. He claims to never say things he does not believe just to get a rise out of people. Since he is out to build a large national audience, he appears to make a conscious effort not to be rude.

Personal Development

So who is Rush Limbaugh and why is he saying all of these things? Rush Hudson Limbaugh, III, born in 1951, was raised in Cape Girardeau, Missouri. He comes from a family of lawyers active in Republican political circles. His grandfather, a lawyer, was ambassador to India during the Eisenhower administration. His uncle was appointed to a federal judgeship by Reagan.[8] His younger brother is a lawyer and handles some of his older brother's legal matters.[9]

The major influence on his political views appears to have been his father. A successful attorney, his father expounded for hours to his sons and their friends on right-wing politics.[10]

While still in high school, Limbaugh's life began to take a turn decidedly away from a career in law. Fascinated by radio and its power, he became a Top-40 disc jockey. He thought that being a radio celebrity would help him romantically. It did not. But once having been bitten by the radio bug, he has found himself in radio almost ever since, except for a five-year stint in the sales office of the Kansas City Royals baseball organization.

Radio has not always been kind to Rush, however. His remarks before or after records got him into trouble with station managers. By his count, he was fired seven times.

Limbaugh dropped out of college after a disappointing freshman year and left for a radio job in Pittsburgh, thwarting his father's plans for another lawyer in the family. Fearful of what would become of him, his father warned Rush what a lack of social standing could mean in life.[11] As Limbaugh went from job to job in Top-40 radio, it must have seemed at times as if his father was right. There are reports of angry confrontations between Limbaugh and his father over the direction of his life.[12]

But talk radio became his road to success, first locally at a station in Sacramento, California, then nationally since 1988, based in New York City. Limbaugh proudly chronicles his transition from local phenomenon to mega-stardom in the early chapters of *The Way Things Ought To Be*.

Shortly before his death, the elder Limbaugh realized his son had finally arrived at a successful career when he saw his son on ABC's *Nightline* in November of 1990. He had been concerned that his son's flippant attitude on the air detracted from his political message. But here he was on a major network television show, offering serious opinion on the troop build-up before the Persian Gulf War. His mother told him his father wondered where he got all that wisdom. He was clearly proud of his son. Limbaugh wrote later, in his book, that his father had been the source.[13]

Along the way to success Limbaugh has gone through two marriages, both ending in divorce, failures for which he seems willing to shoulder the blame. Living alone in New York, he has not given up hope of finding another mate. He has been looking for someone who is successful in her own right and does not need a total togetherness relationship with him.[14]

Although Limbaugh claims to be nothing more than an entertainer, he is far more. He effectively communicates a conservative political worldview day after day.

His way of looking at the world, people and government is of interest to the Christian believer. It would be difficult to determine just how many evangelical and fundamentalist Christians tune in to Rush Limbaugh on a regular basis. According to one report, advertisers estimate that 20 to 25 percent of his 20 million weekly audience is made up of such believers.[15]

A look at this secular prophet of the political right to see how his views relate to the message of the Bible is in order.

---

[1]Maureen O'Brien, "Limbaugh Signs Second Deal with Pocket Books for 'Several Million,'" *Publishers Weekly*, Feb. 1, 1993, p. 12.

[2]*RLRS*, July 1, 1993.

[3]*RLRS*, June 10, 1993.

[4]Ronald Reagan, letter dated December 11, 1992, in

"Rush News," *LL*, Vol. 2, No. 2, Feb. 1993, p. 8.

Dear Rush:

Thanks for all you're doing to promote Republican and conservative principles. Now that I've retired from active politics, I don't mind that you've become the number one voice for conservatism in our country.

I know the liberals call you "the most dangerous man in America," but don't worry about it, they used to say the same thing about me. Keep up the good work! America needs to hear "the way things ought to be."

Sincerely,

(signed) Ron

[5]Rush H. Limbaugh, III, *The Way Things Ought To Be*, (New York: Pocket Books, 1992), p. 22.

[6]Ibid., p. 21.

[7]*RLRS*, July 8, 1993.

[8]Peter J. Boyer, "Bull Rush," *Vanity Fair*, May 1992, p. 205.

[9]*RL*, p. 8.

[10]Boyer, p. 206.

[11]Ibid.

[12]Steven V. Roberts, "What a Rush!" *U.S. News & World Report*, August 16, 1993, p. 31.

[13]*RL*, p. 17.

[14]Boyer, p. 208.

[15]Roy Maynard, "Can We Talk?" *World*, July 17, 1993, p. 12.

There are staged bits [in the television show], such as hidden-camera footage of a Bill Clinton look-alike swiping copies of "The Way Things Ought To Be" from the Limbaugh library. It sounds dumb. It is dumb. But it has a loose geniality that undercuts the spectre of Rush Limbaugh as direct pipeline to the political unconscious.

James Wolcott, *The New Yorker*

The nation doesn't need healing. It needs the truth. Which I am, of course, happy to supply.

LL

I combine irreverence and a sense of humor with serious discussion. Nowhere else does that happen. If Johnny Carson came out and tried to tell you what he really thought about something, you'd get nervous. If Ted Koppel opened with a comedy monologue, [you'd think] "Uh-oh, something's wrong here." With me, people get both.

Rush Limbaugh, *U.S. News & World Report*

**Rush Limbaugh
and the Bible**

2

Is Laughter the Best Medicine for a Sick Society?

*L*ampooning public figures and institutions has a long tradition in America. Political satire has a long history in Western civilization. Rush Limbaugh taps into that stream and turns it in a politically conservative direction.

Right-wing political sentiments have not usually been couched in humorous language. Nor has moralizing generally been conducted by getting people to laugh. As a result, Limbaugh's use of humor can come as quite a surprise to the system.

Of course, Americans have become used to their government officials and institutions being laughed about. Certain Hollywood productions in times past have challenged them. The Marx Brothers' comedy, *Duck Soup* (1933), creates the mythical countries of Freedonia and Sylvania and targets political leaders and war by being hilariously absurd. Charlie Chaplin's *The Great Dictator* (1940) ridiculed Hitler and fascism with scathing preciseness. *Dr. Strangelove (Or, How I Learned to Stop Worrying and Love the Bomb)* (1964) even made black comedy about the end of the world, with an insane general triggering an unstoppable nuclear holocaust. A simpleton is mistakenly assumed to be a political genius in *Being There* (1979).

Television has produced its share of political satire. Some of it has been through showcasing stand-up comedians who weave political jokes into their routines. Situation comedies have occasionally had fun at a political figure's expense.

Through the years comedians have produced records and tapes of political satire or parody. Recording artists have released songs that question the integrity of, or poke fun at, political or national figures. Political cartoons and cartoon strips have scored points or provided a chuckle in the sobering parade of daily events.

One show, NBC's *Saturday Night Live*, perhaps

more and for a longer period of time than any other, has made fun of political institutions. Parodies of presidents, take-offs on political leaders and news items showing the foibles of our leaders have been a steady feature during its nearly 20-year history. When a president was prone to trip, or to verbally slip, or was subject to an embarrassing illness, he was likely to see it highlighted on Saturday late night television. If a senator, congressman, governor, mayor or other official had done something awkward or was touched by scandal, he or she became fair game for satire. Limbaugh seems to have taken his cue from some of the features of *Saturday Night Live* in producing his own television show. Both productions flaunt the same spirit of irreverence toward all political figures.

Was all of this simply humor and entertainment? Behind most satire there has been a particular political persuasion. Much of it came from the left. Often the artists were pushing at the limits of acceptability. If there was any political message, it was in the joke, the routine or the sketch itself.

Rush's Use of Humor

Rush Limbaugh's use of humor is a two-pronged approach. He deftly uses humor and state-of-the-art entertainment both to get across political messages and to prepare the way for his political monologue. The monologue then reinforces the message he has already begun through the use of humor.

His "Updates" are routines that cleverly use comedy to both transmit a message and to set the tone for what will follow. A good example is his "Animal Rights Updates." These are always heralded by his use of an adulterated recording of Andy Williams' rendition of the song "Born Free." This gentle theme song from a movie about an endangered lion, is turned on its head through the over-dubbing of sounds of gunfire and animal screams. Limbaugh, having secured his listener's attention, then proceeds to challenge the idea that even animals have rights. He generally finds an example of a current effort to save an endangered species or to protect a creature's natural habitat. He questions which is more important: human progress or the supposed rights of animals.

The humor does not stop when the "Update" theme music stops. The music introduction sets the tone. First-time listeners and even faithful fans are put in a mood. This is off-beat. This is funny. Limbaugh then continues to use the mood to call into question a cause others take to be serious.

"Up, Up and Away (In My Beautiful Balloon)" introduces "Condom Updates," "Homeless Updates" begin with the song, "I Ain't Got No Home." A chorus of chain saws playing a blues song, guitar-style, while voices shout "Timber!" and trees crash to the ground, ushers in "Timber Updates." The song sets the "Updates" off from the rest of the show. But more than that, its purpose is to create the idea that what follows is too way-out to be believed. "You'll never guess what these crazy people want to do now. . . ." People holding the view in question are not going to be taken seriously.

The Use of the Absurd

Limbaugh's use of humor goes a step further as he challenges "absurdity by being absurd." Interwoven in a radio or television monologue he will present an idea or a plan that is absolutely absurd. Yet this absurd proposal is spoken of in a serious manner. Thrown into the mix of ideas and thoughtful commentary is this totally ludicrous idea. The listener asks, "Was Rush serious? Did he say what I thought he said?" Limbaugh says that he uses these "absurdities" to train his audience not to accept uncritically everything they hear or read, even what proceeds from his own lips or pen.[1]

One example of the use of the absurd, reproduced in *The Way Things Ought To Be*, was first done on April Fool's Day, which should have been a fairly obvious tip-off that something was up. In a serious monologue about the rising federal deficit, Limbaugh proposed taxing the poor since they were the ones not pulling their weight and since America has "the richest poor people in the world." If people were really serious about cutting the deficit, this odd proposal of taxing the poor might sound realistic. Indeed it did. A number of people called because they thought he was serious.[2] Quite to the contrary, he was demonstrating the absurdity of removing money from people's hands to give it to the government to spend for them. It was used to reinforce his point that more money ought to be left in private hands.

Another example occurred in a discussion of the tax policy of President John F. Kennedy. Limbaugh played portions of a speech given by Kennedy at the Economic Club of New York in December, 1962, in which Kennedy said that taxes should be reduced if growth in the economy is to be spurred. Afterwards, Limbaugh claimed that if John Kennedy were alive he would be a "dittohead"—an avid supporter of Limbaugh's point of view.[3] Such a claim, intended to needle liberals, causes laughter because it calls into question the established public image of a liberal past-president. Kennedy, an icon of liberalism, is being claimed by Limbaugh as a compatriot 30 years after his assassination because of one area of convergence in their economic views. It is, of course, the height of absurdity.

New vistas for humor have been made available with the introduction of *Rush Limbaugh: The Television Show.* For the most part the material is a distillation of what was dealt with in the radio show produced and aired earlier in the day. Unlike the radio show, however, there is an audience in the studio during the taping of each TV program. The addition of an audience changes the dynamics. Limbaugh plays off their reactions to his comments. He is often spurred on to say more or to go a little further in the direction he was already headed. Their laughter and applause, as with any public performance, has its effect on the final product.

Visual Comedy

The sight of Limbaugh sitting at a desk, in front of a live audience, dispensing political and social commentary, adds the visual dimension of comedy. On radio he is a voice and comedy involves sound alone. On television his facial expressions can tip the viewer off as to how he means a statement. A raised eyebrow, a grimace, a rolling of the eyes, a sideways glance, a blown kiss, a goodbye wave can color the message. Facial expressions, gestures and tone of voice can undercut a quotation from a speech he disagrees with. The studio and television audience are telegraphed a cue as to what Limbaugh really thinks about the material he is dealing with. Nonverbals combine with verbal communication to make clear what he finds mildly amusing, utterly ridiculous, downright absurd or disgustingly contemptible.

Limbaugh has an expressive face and uses it to comic advantage. His voice has an air of confidence and authority about it. Combined on television, both are skillfully handled tools used to poke fun at liberalism. One standard technique is to show a film clip of a portion of someone's speech or press conference and then interrupt it with his interpretation and analysis. Sometimes he will begin laughing merely at the sight of certain opponents. Often he mimics the

speaker's voice. Other times he will not official-
ly interrupt the film clip. Instead, a superimposed box with his face in it will appear in the
lower left corner of the television screen. Looking up at the speaker he will make faces, shake
his head, laugh, gesture and carry-on, holding
his opponent up to ridicule even while he or
she speaks. It is a form of heckling after the fact.
The studio audience always erupts with
laughter. The speaker, on film or tape or being
quoted, of course is helpless to defend himself.

Rush's Fairness Doctrine

Is Limbaugh fair to the opposition? No! But he
never claims to be. Feeling that he is doing battle with the liberal-dominated popular press in a
struggle in which conservatives are badly out-
numbered, he has apparently concluded that
any tactic is fair. He may be taking cheap shots,
but they work. His growing ratings apparently
mean that his radio and television audiences
love to see him bash liberals, without the other
side being able to talk back.

By setting himself up as the outgunned under-
dog fighting against immense odds to get the
truth out to the people, Limbaugh has the
audience pulling for him. When he scores a hit
on one of his targets the crowd cheers. He has
created an image of himself as the champion of
truth in a deceitful world, the paragon of virtue
in a wicked era. If he should appear unfair to
the opposition, well, that's okay. After all, they
are the opposition and they very much have the

media on their side. Like a knight in shining armor, he is fighting on the side of good and decency.

Does humor keep Limbaugh from being taken seriously? A satirical swipe might get a laugh, but does it prove effective in getting a point across?

Is humor the best medicine for a sick society? Limbaugh uses humor not only as an entertainment element to keep his audience's attention, but also to make his points. Sometimes the point may get lost in the humor. Other times the humor drives home the point. Consequently, the mood of his shows, both radio and television, is always upbeat. Even in the period immediately following the Republican loss of the White House after 12 years, he was optimistic. He remains full of hope for the future even when circumstances are depressing.[4]

Contagious Joy

His excitement and joy are contagious. They come across to his audience. This inner joy and his upbeat nature seem to stem from a confidence that his views are right and will someday triumph. Limbaugh's message of hope inspires his fans to believe that change for the better is possible. So the humor fits the hopeful message. They go hand in hand. Since he so strongly believes his views are correct, he feels free to unhesitatingly criticize the opposition through ridicule. He, thereby, builds added confidence in his audience's mind that he knows whereof he speaks. With Rush, humor is certainly no laughing matter. It is a powerful channel of communication.

Bible-believing Christians can identify with Limbaugh's long-term optimism. Right will win in the end. Even though it may look as though wrong is in control, truth will have its day. Even though things seem gloomy now, keep the faith; God will see His purposes accomplished in the end. When Limbaugh attacks what his followers perceive to be the forces of evil by ridiculing them, they applaud and cheer. Dispairing of turning society around and correcting the imbalance of evil over good, short of Divine intervention, this loyal vanguard is encouraged when so vocal and visible a force for traditional values as Rush Limbaugh can get in a few licks for the cause of decency.

---

[1] *RL*, p. 29.

[2] Ibid., pp. 36–43.

[3] *RLRS*, June 30, 1993.

[4] Rush Limbaugh, "Let the Good Times Roll," *LL*, Vol. 1, No. 3, Dec. 1992, p. 1.

Certainly if any conservative is in line to inherit [from Ronald Reagan] the mantle of "The Great Communicator," it is the idol of the "dittoheads."

James Bowman, *National Review*

Banning prayer in school in effect made God unconstitutional.

RL

The Not So Silent Majority

*W*hy does the message of Rush Limbaugh resonate in the evangelical Christian community? Why do so many seem ready to join forces with him? We must examine some background material before we understand the support Limbaugh finds among Bible-believing Christians.

Evangelical Christians today seem ready to enlist in the battle to save America from the forces of secular humanism. Some of them are finding in Rush Limbaugh a fellow-soldier, if not a general. Someone to lead the charge against pro-abortion feminists, soft-on-crime liberals and out-of-the-closet gays who are perceived threats to the "American way of life."

Readiness to do open battle against societal ills has not always been the case for Evangelicals. Since the turn of the 20th century, evangelicalism has undergone a metamorphosis.

Evangelical Protestant Christianity was once the dominant culture-shaping force in American society. The 19th century has been hailed as the era of a Protestant America. Clergymen were highly respected and held vast power in the cities and towns of this country. The Sunday morning sermon was the intellectual and spiritual apex of the week.

Evangelical congregants could be found not only in church on Sunday but active in their faith throughout the week. The "Benevolent Empire," a network of Protestant, non-denominational charitable organizations combated alcoholism, slavery, prostitution and other social ills. Evangelicalism, though revivalistic and pietistic, was also active in seeking to make this world a better place by reforming society. This reformism was a side effect of an active Christian faith. A personal relationship with God through a salvation experience grounded in the atoning death of Christ was foundational. Personal salvation was crucial for every individual.

The Rise of Liberalism

Toward the end of the 19th century, liberal forces arose within American Protestantism that turned from belief in the traditional orthodox Christian doctrines. Many liberal Protestants shifted the emphasis away from personal salvation toward an effort to redeem society. The Social Gospel was a movement away from seeing individual man as sinful and in need of personal salvation. Social Gospel preachers pointed to societal evil and called on individuals to join together and, with God's help, eradicate the evil forces that were at work in corporate society. Evil forces in society were seen as corrupting the individual. Humans were essentially good. Society was evil.

These advocates of social reform undertook to clear slums, to end child labor practices and to eliminate a host of other social evils. They put a major emphasis on education. If society could be redeemed humankind could create a perfect habitat here on this earth.

Reacting to the Social Gospel and modernism's attacks on orthodox Christian beliefs, evangelical Protestants rallied around fundamental doctrines of the faith. The issuance of *The Fundamentals*, a series of books defending traditional Christian teachings, shortly after the start of the 20th century, gave Evangelicals a new name, Fundamentalists.

Fundamentalists distanced themselves from liberal Protestantism. They defended the long-held doctrines of the virgin birth of Christ, biblical miracles, the vicarious death of Christ for human sin, the physical resurrection of Christ from the dead and the imminent, literal return of Jesus Christ to rapture His saints and establish His millennial reign. These central beliefs were undergirded by a strong belief in the inerrancy of God's Word, the Bible.

A full-scale battle ensued. Colleges, seminaries and denominations that had once been bastions of evangelicalism were taken over by the forces of modernism. Modernism's rejection of the core beliefs of traditional Christianity and skepticism about the truth of the Bible opened a yawning gulf between Fundamentalists and Modernists. The social activism of 19th century Evangelicals gave way to the social withdrawal of 20th century Fundamentalists, as Evangelicals separated themselves from religious institutions they deemed to be apostate.

Withdrawal meant the establishment of Bible-believing churches, denominations, colleges, seminaries and mission boards. It also meant separation from the world. Personal holiness was prized. One could become contaminated from contact with the evil world, so the best course of action, whenever possible, was social isolation. Gathering inside the four walls of their churches, fundamentalist believers worried more about preparation for the next world than they did any social work in this already condemned world. Self-preservation, keeping the true faith, seemed to demand strict separation.

Losing the Larger Battle

The Scopes Trial in 1925 accelerated the process of withdrawal and separation. The so-called "Monkey Trial" pitted evolution and biblical creationism against each other. H.L. Mencken and others in the secular press heaped ridicule upon the Fundamentalists. Creationists won the court case in Dayton, Tennessee, but Fundamentalists lost the larger battle. The press-generated image of the Fundamentalist as a backwoods ignoramus was locked indelibly in the American consciousness.

Withdrawing from the mainstream of society over the following several decades, American Fundamentalists built their own institutions and grew in numbers. The focus was on soul-winning and preparation for Christ's impending return. Certain defining lifestyle rules regulated both their behavior and dress.

But not all Fundamentalists were comfortable with the label and the extreme rigidity it connoted. Nor were they comfortable with a mind-set that had virtually ceded the church's social ministries to liberals. Post-World War II American Protestantism was further split with the founding in 1942 of the National Association of Evangelicals. The publication of Carl F.H. Henry's *The Uneasy Conscience of Modern Fundamentalism* (1947) added impetus to evangelicalism as did the later founding of *Christianity Today* magazine.

Evangelical Christians were prepared to reenter the mainstream of American society.

Many Fundamentalists, however, were more than content to remain isolated and separated. They viewed evangelicalism, with which they shared basic core doctrinal beliefs, critically. They saw Evangelicals as compromisers, willing to work in the social arena with liberal Protestants. They considered their lifestyle regulations as too relaxed. Deep rifts began to develop between Fundamentalists, who still maintained a combative attitude, and Evangelicals, who were seeking the respect of society-at-large.

The Rise of Political Involvement

The prospect of a Roman Catholic occupant in the White House gave Fundamentalists and Evangelicals a brief common cause. Fearing rule by the Vatican, both voted in substantial numbers against Kennedy and for Nixon. It was a losing effort for both kinds of beliefs.

The 1960s brought many changes in American society that were unsettling to religiously conservative Protestants. The public school system was the stage for some of these. In 1962 the Supreme Court ruled that recital of a prescribed prayer in public schools was unconstitutional. The following year the court ruled that Bible reading in public schools was likewise unconstitutional. Long since, the theory of evolution had displaced creationism in the science classrooms of most public schools.

Even in the face of these faith-threatening developments, evangelical and fundamentalist

Protestants were slow to become politically involved. With the exception of the 1960 presidential election, Evangelicals and Fundamentalists did not begin to become politically active in any significant numbers until the founding of the Moral Majority in 1979. Until that point in time they were part of the "silent majority" that provided Richard Nixon's base of support in 1968 and 1972. Supportive of law and order, leery of feminism, opposed to the freewheeling lifestyle of the 1960s hippie generation and critical of the rapid social changes underway, the silent majority longed for stability, a return to solid family values.

In the wake of Watergate, the election of a Democrat in 1976 was assured. Jimmy Carter, ex-governor of Georgia and a born-again Southern Baptist Sunday school teacher, won the White House. He appeared to be a president who would please religiously conservative Protestants. Instead, he was a disappointment. Not only was he too liberal politically for most conservatives, but the taking of American hostages by Iran, Carter's inability to negotiate their release and the aborted military effort to free them resulted in low morale not only in the White House but across America. High interest rates, caused in large part by Arab oil embargoes, further undercut confidence in Carter's leadership, both domestically and in foreign policy.

The "Religious Right"

Enter the Moral Majority. Founded in 1979 by

the Reverend Jerry Falwell, a fundamentalist Baptist pastor and Christian television personality, the Moral Majority rallied politically conservative fundamentalist and evangelical Christians. The Moral Majority sought to educate and mobilize the conservative masses to support morally upright candidates for public office. Speaking out against abortion, pornography, drug use, homosexuality and the Equal Rights Amendment, it wanted to reverse the trend of society toward immorality, hence its name. Favoring government vouchers and choice in education, the death penalty, putting prayer back in the schools, the protection of human life in the womb and a strong military, it was responding to the social upheaval in America by digging in its heels and saying no to unbridled liberalism. Based on its direct mailing list, it estimated nearly four million adherents. Chapters of the Moral Majority were established in all 50 states. At every stage, critics in the popular media attacked it for attempting to enact into law a particular religious viewpoint.

When Ronald Reagan came along to lead the conservative wing of the Republican Party to victory, he found strong support among Moral Majority adherents. (Somewhere along the line the media labeled them "the Religious Right.") The importance of their support for Reagan in his capture of the White House in 1980 and 1984 has been the subject of much study. One thing is clear, the Republican Party benefited from the mobilization of voters by the Religious

Right. Reagan, and Bush after him, personally verbalized, and the Republican Party platform articulated, core social beliefs dear to the hearts of the Religious Right. As a direct result, Republican candidates received their votes in significant numbers.

The dissolution of the Moral Majority took place in 1989. Jerry Falwell announced that the organization would be phased out of existence. Falwell had concluded that it had served its purpose. It had established the Religious Right as a force in the shaping of public policy.

Another organization soon filled the gap. Pat Robertson, head of the largest and most successful Christian radio and cable TV network, attempted to gain the 1988 Republican nomination for president. When that failed, his followers began the Christian Coalition. Picking up where the Moral Majority left off, this coalition of concerned Christians began organizing, on a grass-roots level, to see that its type of candidates will gain the nomination on all levels of Republican politics. So far the Coalition's success has been significant enough to cause concern among some traditional party regulars. The Christian Coalition has faced the same bad press that dogged the Moral Majority. Its adherents are called intolerant extremists by the popular media.

The Liberal Evangelicals

A small but articulate number of Evangelicals falls into the category of politically liberal social activists. In the early 1970s a group of Evangelicals, mainly students at the time, began to advocate a radical form of Christian discipleship. The Sojourner Community proposed the sharing of material goods with the poor and a compassionate use of wealth. Through its magazine and the books of Jim Wallis and Ron Sider, the Sojourner Community has influenced evangelicalism. Harkening back to 19th century Protestantism, this group feels it is being true to the teachings of Jesus Christ by speaking out against materialism, racial oppression and government policies that adversely impact the poor. Active supporters are numerically smaller and, therefore, less prominent than the Religious Right.

While allowing for shades of political and social awareness, decidedly more Evangelicals and Fundamentalists, as a whole, would fall into the conservative than the liberal political camp. At no point are they more united than in the support for traditional family values.

The Rush to Rush

Anyone, therefore, who articulates support for the family and appears to be against the forces that would lead the nation further into immorality, has a fertile segment of the population already predisposed to his support. When someone comes over the airwaves denouncing political liberalism, supporting belief in God, attacking evolution and defending the Judeo-Christian framework of society, he will find a corps of encouragers.

It is no secret that American society is deeply fragmented. In this chapter we've seen some of the religio-social forces that have shaped late-20th century Evangelicals and Fundamentalists. These forces, coupled with the political and social changes in the last 30 or 40 years, have led to a "cultural war." While most Evangelicals and Fundamentalists might not support everything that Rush Limbaugh says, or they may wish he would have said it in a different way, nonetheless they see him as a leader in the battle over America's future direction.

When Vice President Dan Quayle addressed the Republican National Convention in Houston, Texas, in August of 1992, he spoke about this "cultural war." Calling attention to the importance of family values, he asserted, "The gap between us and our opponents is a cultural divide. It's not just a difference between conservative and liberal. It is a difference between fighting for what is right and refusing to see what is wrong."[1] Clearly, for Quayle, there are moral absolutes. Rather than "anything goes" there are right and wrong actions, attitudes and lifestyles. He placed himself, and his party, on the side of traditional family values.

The other side would counter-argue that individual freedom dictates an open attitude toward those who might not see the value of moral laws. They would hold that codes of interpersonal conduct that have been handed down from past centuries need not be seen as valid through all time. They would advocate tolerance for those who differ from long-established patterns of behavior. Conservatives object. There *are* values. They *are* important. Moral values form the very fabric of society.

When former presidential candidate Pat Buchanan spoke to the Republican National Convention in 1992, he made himself quite clear. "There is a religious war going on in this country for the soul of America," he charged. "It is a cultural war as critical to the kind of nation we shall be as the Cold War itself, for this war is for the soul of America."[2] Buchanan's equating the importance of the "cultural war" with the Cold War shows just how crucial the conservative side sees the struggle. Just as trillions of dollars and strenuous effort were put into fighting world communism, so conservative leaders are calling for strong effort to be mounted to win the current "cultural war." They feel that the very future of America is at stake.

The battle lines have been drawn. Conservative forces have arrayed themselves against the forces of secular humanism. Secular humanism is defined as the view of the world which places ultimate value on the development of humanity to the exclusion of any divine influence. God is seen as either nonexistent or irrelevant to life on earth.

When Rush Limbaugh speaks out for traditional values, when he holds up liberal positions to public ridicule, when he vocalizes the felt needs of the "silent majority," he assumes a prophetic role. Being attacked by liberal critics only serves to validate his role as a prophet.

Old Testament prophets often were not valued by the political establishment. Many found themselves exiled, some were killed. Limbaugh's fate is quite different. Reviled by his critics, he is revered by his faithful audience. Known affectionately as "dittoheads," (Limbaugh asks callers-in to shorten their adulation of him to the word *ditto*), these enthusiasts have made him a radio phenomenon. In the process he has become financially well-off.

Christians are attracted to Limbaugh because of his defense of traditional values. They are not always pleased with his choice of words, nor do they find all of his humor entirely to their liking. But when compared to the dominant news organizations in the country many Bible-believing Christians choose to trust Rush Limbaugh as their source for opinion on the current events of the day. They see him as on their side in the war for America's future. He gives them bulletins from the front lines, intelligence reports on the "enemy" and pep talks to encourage them when everything seems to be going wrong.

Just where does Rush Limbaugh stand on the key issues of this "cultural war?" What positions has he set forth? What specifically does he oppose? How does all of this fit into the biblically based positions held by Evangelicals and Fundamentalists in America today? Let's move on to examine some issues.

[1]Dan Quayle, "The Family Comes First: We Cannot Take Orders from Special Interests," a speech delivered at the Republican National Convention, Houston, Texas, August 20, 1992, *Vital Speeches of the Day*, Sept. 15, 1992, p. 711.

[2]Pat Buchanan, "The Election Is About Who We Are: Taking Back Our Country," a speech delivered at the Republican National Convention, Houston, Texas, August 17, 1992, *Vital Speeches of the Day*, Sept. 15, 1992, p. 714.

And, half-improvised as every half-hour [of the television show] is . . . Limbaugh always manages, just like a good lecturer or a good tent-preacher, to bring his final point home with just the right solemnity, earnestness, and half-octave drop in the voice.

Frank McConnell, *Commonweal*

But you can't teach The Ten Commandments because that stems from somebody's religion.

RLTS

The people were flocking to their new prophet in amazing numbers. . . . One by one, local stations jumped on the Limbaugh band-wagon—by July 1990, 244 had signed up to hear the Gospel According to Rush.

Michael Arkush, *Rush!*

4

The Gospel According to Rush

*I*t is Rush Limbaugh's firm belief that America was built on a Judeo-Christian foundation. He admits that the role of religious belief in the history of this country is not taught in our schools today and he feels it should be.[1] He affirms his personal belief in "one God" and holds that this country was established with belief in God at the core of its founding principles.[2]

Unfortunately, anti-religious forces have

worked in this country to remove prayer and Bible reading from the classroom. Crowding religion out of public life, Supreme Court decisions have narrowed the rights of those who wish to practice their religion in public places.

The public arena is the main focus of Limbaugh's comments on religion. That is where he sees a real battle underway. What he labels an "assault" is being made upon the religious foundations of the nation. The dispute has centered around how to interpret the First Amendment of the Constitution. The separation of church and state, he maintains, was not set forth by this country's founders to protect the people from religion, but from government's trying to establish one religion over others.[3] He strongly objects to interpretations of the First Amendment which seek to remove religion from active inclusion in the public life of the nation. In his view this was not the intention of the framers of the Constitution.

Bringing Back Religion

Limbaugh is in favor of bringing religion back into America's classrooms. Like many others, he wonders if it is only a coincidence that the quality of education has been in decline since the expression of religion began to be removed from schools 30 years ago.[4]

He rejoiced when the Supreme Court ruled that religious groups must be allowed to use school property after hours, just as any other group can. Limbaugh hailed the Supreme Court decision allowing prayer at commencement ceremonies, if led by students and not clergy. He called it a victory for the faithful and God-fearing.[5]

In discussing with a 17-year-old caller how being created by God is the basis of self-worth, he wondered what an atheist would base his or her self-worth on. He encouraged him to read Pascal's *Pensees*, assuring the caller that Pascal's efforts to prove the existence of God would send tingles up and down his back.[6]

He wonders why creationism cannot be taught in schools, since it comes from God. It takes faith to believe in creationism, he told his radio audience. Yet, Limbaugh notes, no one has been able to prove cross-specie evolution, which must be accepted by faith. It puzzles him that faith in God is deemed wrong, whereas faith in science is all right.[7] This faith in humanity rather than God raises questions for Limbaugh about the ultimate value of human life. He told his listeners that although it was an impossibility for humans to actually succeed in creating life, if they think they can create life out of nothing there is a reduction in the value of life.[8]

The origin and sanctity of human life matters. The Bible clearly teaches that God began life and that human destiny is in His control. Advances in medical science have made tremendous changes in the treatment of the human body. There are limits, however, to human knowledge. Matters of life and death are still in

God's hands, not humankind's. The notion that all mysteries will be worked out by human intellectual development leads to a man-centered view that excludes the Creator from the picture.

One of the reasons many Evangelicals and Fundamentalists are attracted to Limbaugh is the fact that he takes God's existence to be an important truth. God's creation of human life has implications which impact how we view ourselves, others and all of life. This is something that appears to be lost to most of the rest of the media establishment. As they see it, religion is a peripheral matter. Limbaugh sees religion as an important builder of society, strengthening values like character and morality.

This fundamental belief in the existence of God and the importance of religion permeates Limbaugh's attitude toward humankind in relation to nature and the animal world and his attitude toward religion's role in fostering morality, as we will note in future chapters.

Because Limbaugh calls to attention the religious heritage of our country and calls for a more active role for religion in today's society, he finds supporters in the Religious Right. This is evidenced, among other ways, by whom he appeared with at a Republican National Coalition for Life event, held in conjunction with the Republican National Convention in Houston in August, 1992. Pat Robertson, Jerry Falwell and Phyllis Schlafly, all longtime prominent leaders of the Religious Right, shared the platform with him at this celebration of the pro-life plank in the Republican Party platform. They share with him the agenda of moving the country in a conservative direction politically. But does he share their theological commitment?

Social Implications

The "gospel" that Rush Limbaugh preaches is heavy on the societal implications of religion and light on a theology of personal redemption. He appears to be vastly more interested in renewing and redeeming society than in personal salvation. He does not discuss religion as religion on his radio or television shows, reportedly because he does not want his shows to be categorized as religious talk shows. It is asserted that he has confessed over the air more than once to being a Christian.[9] It is also reported that he seldom goes to church.[10]

The message Limbaugh presents is theologically incomplete. He trumpets the role religion has played in the shaping of our nation's founding documents and history. He notes that belief in God is important. But teaching that America's founders were religious and that one should believe in God will not get at the core of the human problem. Important as our religious roots and belief in God are, standing alone they are insufficient to remedy man's malady. The fundamental issue of human sin must be dealt with on an individual basis by repentance for sin and acceptance of salvation through Jesus Christ the Lord.

The role of religion that Limbaugh points to is

as the teacher of morals and values. While some of our moral standards come from the Bible, he told his radio audience, other moral standards have developed over the centuries. They were not merely imposed by the brute force of the majority, but developed because certain standards worked best. Morality cannot be defined by the individual, he added, otherwise there are no standards.[11] So, religion is to be supported primarily for what it does for society. It provides moral undergirding. An attack upon religion or a lessening of the area of free-reign for religion in public life is seen as a threat to the moral fabric of the nation.

Limbaugh makes the charge that many liberals are out to remove religion not only from our history but from all of our public institutions.[12] Religion, that helped to form this country, is not to be allowed in "liberal America," he said on the radio, therefore, liberals want to come up with their own religion to transmit their values.[13] In *The Way Things Ought To Be*, he identifies that substitute religion as secular humanist philosophy coupled with belief in the state.[14]

The message that secular humanism teaches is that we need no outside help. Our own intelligence and strength are sufficient. Certainly this teaching clearly runs counter to the teaching of the Bible that God has acted in history on our behalf. In making humanity the focus of attention, secular humanism displaces God. There is no place for the Creator in His world.

We are good enough on our own. Sin is not a problem. Some of us might do bad things, but we are not really evil. We are basically good. There is no need therefore for salvation, no need for a Christ to redeem us. Those who advocate this view appear to be winning the day in America. They seem to be successfully convincing many that we really do not need God.

There Is Danger, Though

It is refreshing and reassuring to hear someone reaffirm belief in God. When Limbaugh highlights the importance of religion and belief in God, we take notice. There is a danger, though. The gospel that Limbaugh presents is a truncated gospel. It is a gospel that sees what religion can do to modify social behavior but stops there.

We are warned in Galatians that people will come along with "false gospels" (Galatians 1:6–9). Obviously, secular humanism is wrong. However, so is any partial gospel that attempts to reduce the Christian message by seeking to use biblical values merely for their social value alone.

Limbaugh's gospel is a political gospel. He is aggressively laying out a conservative political agenda. His agenda must not be mistaken for the full gospel. Where it supports the Christian message, as found in the Bible, it should be applauded. Where it diverges, it should be judged. We should be cautious about wedding the gospel of Christ to any particular political ideology. God's program is spiritual in nature. While it has political ramifications, if it is reduced only to politics it is neither the true gospel nor God's true mission for His people.

---

[1] *RL*, p. 274.

[2] Ibid., p. 3.

[3] Ibid., pp. 277–281.

[4] Ibid., pp. 275–276.

[5] *RLRS*, June 7, 1993.

[6] *RLRS*, July 2, 1993.

[7] *RLRS*, July 15, 1993.

[8] *RLRS*, July 7, 1993.

[9] Jeff Dunn, "Rush Fever in Christian Stores," *Christian Retailing*, July 1, 1993, p. 28.

[10] Steven V. Roberts, "What a Rush!" *U.S. News & World Report*, August 16, 1993, p. 30.

[11] *RLRS*, July 2, 1993.

[12] *RL*, p. 281.

[13] *RLRS*, July 14, 1993.

[14] *RL*, p. 281.

I'm not antiwoman at all. I love women. In fact, I have a view of women that I think is rooted in respect and a desire to treat a woman in a certain way. You can't say that now. That's sexist. If you disagree with what the feminists want, you must be antiwoman, and you're an arcane dinosaur.

Rush Limbaugh, *U.S. News & World Report*

The self-appointed intellectual aristocracy (and whoever says there is no cultural elite, is one) has been wrong about nearly every cultural idea for at least 30 years.

LL

5

No Wife, No Kids—Is This Man an Expert on Family Values?

*R*ush Limbaugh is a strong supporter of traditional morality. But how does one learn right and wrong? The sources are twofold, according to Limbaugh. Certain rights and wrongs are known instinctively, others are learned in the family setting. Family values include the sense of morality and decency provided by growing up in a good family.[1]

"Family values" has come to mean traditional morality. Barbara Bush articulated her definition of family values at the Republican National Convention in 1992: "As in our family, as in American families everywhere, the parents we've met are determined to teach their children integrity, strength, responsibility, courage, sharing, love of God and pride in being an American. However you define family, that's what we mean by family values."[2]

Since Rush Limbaugh has no children and in 1993 has no wife, critics might ask what makes him an expert on family values? One does not have to experience all of family life personally to understand the importance of family in the building of good citizens. Certainly Limbaugh's upbringing provided him with an understanding of family sufficient for him to speak to the issue.

Growing up in a family involves a socialization process in which one learns to respond to the world in a prescribed manner. All of us bear the marks of growing up. What we are taught, or not taught, during our formative years in the home will influence our steps the rest of our lives.

Family values have traditionally been firmly grounded in absolute moral values. Echoing philosophers and theologians of ages past, Limbaugh notes that the ultimate source of morality is Divine. Our Creator has laws that are not open to tampering or change by man.[3] There is, then, according to Limbaugh, a basis for human morality in the laws of God. This divinely based code of morality has become the foundation of Judeo-Christian civilization. These laws have been handed down to us in the Bible, God's Word.

The biblical account indicates a bond being formed between man and woman for the establishment of the family unit. A man and a woman unite to become one (Genesis 2:24). God has provided the necessary physical equipment to facilitate human reproduction. Children are the natural product of this uniting of male with female.

The divinely ordained pattern is for the parents to train their children in the ways of God. Human conduct is seen to be under Divine supervision. Human acts have both temporal and eternal consequences. The way humans conduct themselves matters. God has designed the family as the nurturing, caring unit to transmit basic rules of behavior.

Morality Rooted in the Divine

When Limbaugh speaks of morality being rooted in our Divine Creator he is affirming an important truth. We are created in the image of God (Genesis 1:27). At least part of what the image of God within us entails is the ability to discern right from wrong. Encoded morality forms the basis of human interaction among normal human beings.

A child's moral development in the family builds upon the sense of oughtness and responsibility given by the Creator. Values learned in the family form the very fabric of human society. Limbaugh warns of the danger of not growing up with the basic laws of human conduct being caringly transmitted. Those who are not raised with these absolute moral values corroborated and built upon, he cautions, are a threat to society.[4]

Even a cursory survey of human history indicates the importance of family values in the survival and development of human society. Prohibitions against murder, marital and sexual regulations, property guidelines and other laws governing conduct, based on the Bible, have provided the tracks upon which the train of Judeo-Christian civilization has run. Rush Limbaugh is one of a long line of defenders of traditional family values who chooses to speak out against forces attempting to tear up the tracks.

The Heart of Limbaugh's Message

Personal responsibility for one's actions is at the heart of Limbaugh's message.[5] This theme echoes and reechoes on his radio and television shows. Whether he is talking about the criminal taking responsibility for his or her crime, a student taking responsibility for his or her education, parents taking responsibility for their child's care, employees taking responsibility for their productivity, his emphasis is upon individual responsibility. If something goes wrong, where does the fault reside? Limbaugh asks us to look inward. While families and forces in society-at-large have a role in shaping human beings, each individual is ultimately accountable for his or her actions. Individuals should take seriously their personal role in determining who they have become and who they are in the process of becoming. Blaming others for one's failures is not Limbaugh's philosophy.

This view of individual responsibility is consistent with biblical teaching. Throughout the Bible, individuals are held responsible for their sins. Even in the Old Testament where corporate Israel was viewed as a unit, capable of national sin, waywardness and repentance, individuals were still accountable for wrong actions. The classic example is King David's sin of taking another man's wife and having that man sent to certain death in battle. David suffered the consequences of his sin. Divine punishment followed (2 Samuel 11–12). David *never* fully regained God's blessing. He was hounded till his death by the consequences of his transgression.

The New Testament teaching is clear as well. Individuals are responsible for their actions. Everyone makes mistakes, no one is perfect (Romans 3:23). The result, however, of doing evil is spiritual death and eternal punishment unless a person repents and secures forgiveness and eternal life through faith in Jesus Christ (Romans 6:23). Wrong actions and attitudes have consequences.

Personal accountability is an essential aspect of a stable society. If individuals shift the blame for their socially unacceptable behavior to others, change for the better will not take place. When whole groups of individuals collectively shirk personal responsibility, society is damaged.

Limbaugh comes down hard on those who refuse to place the blame for criminal actions on individuals who commit crimes. He will not countenance excuses that charge society with guilt for what individuals do. Conditions in one's neighborhood, lack of employment, racial prejudice or other factors cannot excuse the individual. Those in leadership positions who tell people that they cannot help committing criminal acts, since society has dealt them a difficult hand, are, according to Limbaugh, holding back both the individual's and the community's prosperity. Only by emphasizing self-reliance and taking charge of one's destiny, Limbaugh holds, will individuals achieve any success in life.[6]

Similarly, the biblical teaching is that when personal responsibility for wrong is admitted and repentance is made, forgiveness and healing can then take place. Unless personal culpability and guilt is confessed, no correction can be achieved.

The Media Attack on the Family

Limbaugh attacks the forces in the "dominant media culture" in American society that work to tear down or weaken family values. If society is to function effectively, moral values must be reinforced. Limbaugh is critical of all influences that adversely influence the retention of traditional values.

In particular Limbaugh levels criticism against the daytime television talk shows that parade across the screen a constant column of people with perverted lifestyles and try to call it normal behavior. People who commit acts that go against societal sexual mores and espouse lifestyles that deviate from traditional values should not be viewed as normal. Yet the message that certain daytime talk shows send out is that there are no moral absolutes; everything is morally relative. How dare we call any lifestyle alternative abnormal or wrong? These types of shows that attempt to equate all "loving" relationships between individuals as proper he sees as a dangerous influence on society. Limbaugh labels them "unadulterated trash."[7]

Hollywood comes under Limbaugh's censure, mostly for its support of liberal politics, but also for ridiculing normal families, monogamy, heterosexual relationships and belief in God. Hollywood no longer makes many movies that support traditional values and reinforce American institutions.[8]

Rap music lyrics calling for the murder of police officers or the abuse of women and supposed art that depicts, in photographs, two men engaged in homosexual acts creates a stir. Why? Because many people find these things obscene and filthy. Yet, Limbaugh notes, those who challenge the production and broad distribution of these are viewed as opposed to freedom. The artist, they argue, should be free to create. The artist may have the freedom to create, Limbaugh allows, but he challenges the artist's right to display and broadcast these creations, especially if public funds are involved.[9]

Unabridged Hedonism

Protection of family values involves speaking out against the forces that seek, either consciously or unconsciously, to destroy those values. Limbaugh finds that attacks upon critics of unbridled hedonism are simply rationalization on the part of liberals who know that what they are doing is wrong. By making everything "normal" they seek to ease their own feelings of guilt.

To be a defender of traditional values, to seek to limit abnormal behavior, critics of Limbaugh charge, is to be a fascist. Apparently everyone should be free to do anything his or her heart desires. Nothing is really wrong. Just excuse all blame, no one is responsible for his or her actions.[10]

Family values, however, form the very core of a well-running, stable, growing society. If human society is going to continue functioning well, moral values must continue to be fostered in each succeeding generation. Western society did not achieve greatness in a vacuum. The Judeo-Christian tradition provided the moral values that gave a solid foundation for economic growth, advances in knowledge and social development. The central parts of that tradition are the moral imperatives of Scripture. These moral imperatives cannot be swept aside without suffering the consequences. They provide for stability and the framework for a peaceful community. When these moral laws are disregarded, disharmony results. Disharmony causes disruption in society. The whole community is adversely impacted, so individual freedom must be restrained at points for the good of the community. Living in community demands that moral values be upheld. An "anything goes" attitude leads, ultimately, to anarchy.

This dissolution into anarchy is what Limbaugh is seeking to guard against. In this he does not stand alone. People of various backgrounds and faiths stand with him in defense of family values. Certainly Evangelicals and Fundamentalists support the basic moral values upon which our society has been constructed. Their desire is to see these values instilled within every generation. While personal faith in Christ on the part of humanity would more easily facilitate a moral society, we should applaud anything that is in support of basic values.

Sex Education

Sex education that merely hands out condoms to school-aged young people and explains the "mechanics" of reproduction more as a disease preventative measure than as preparatory to meaningful sexual development, is inadequate. Rush Limbaugh has repeatedly urged that the teaching of abstinence be made a part of sex education programs. He argues that it is the only 100 per cent sure way to avoid both disease and pregnancy. That more school systems do not teach abstinence is discouraging. Limbaugh joins with those who see abstinence as something that can be taught, something that is effective and something that would help to build character in young lives.

Since the teaching of abstinence would be teaching an inhibition of activity, it is opposed by those who see total personal freedom as the condition to be maintained at all times. To tell one not to do something goes against the grain of a permissive society. But abstinence from sexual activity prior to marriage is the clear teaching of the Bible.

Government Cannot Instill Values

The task of instilling values cannot be effectively done by government.[11] Limbaugh apparently feels that even well-intended government programs fail to provide the conditions necessary to teach children family values. The way to build a moral society is to have strong families passing along to the next generation the moral values that have made our society and Judeo-Christian civilization great.

While government should not be entrusted with the job of instilling family values, obviously government programs can impact families. Government programs which support the family are positive factors; those that weaken the family are negative factors. Any program which makes it financially advantageous for one of the parents to be absent from the home harms the family unit and weakens the moral structure of the country.

Limbaugh understands and articulates the

basic truth that American society has its foundation in absolute moral values derived from the Judeo-Christian Scriptures. He knows that our civil laws go back to these roots. If the absolute moral laws are transgressed, personal and societal harm results. Disharmony and conflict can be avoided only if society remains on the solid footing of traditional moral values. In the current permissive atmosphere in America created by moral relativism and secular humanistic understanding of human life, Limbaugh's reaffirmation of moral absolutes is to be applauded. Family values must be defended and upheld if our society is to function properly.

---

[1]Rush Limbaugh, "The Culture War," *LL*, Vol. 2, No. 1, Jan. 1993, p. 10.

[2]Barbara Bush, "Family Values: The Country's Future Is in Your Hands," a speech delivered at the Republican National Convention, Houston, Texas, August 19, 1992, *Vital Speeches of the Day*, Sept. 15, 1992.

[3]*RL*, p. 3.

[4]*LL*, "The Culture War," p. 10.

[5]*RL*, p. 49.

[6]Ibid., pp. 220–222.

[7]*RLRS*, July 8, 1993.

[8]*RL*, p. 254.

[9]*LL*, "The Culture War," p. 10.

[10]Ibid.

[11]*RL*, p. 2.

Still, the secret to America is not fairness, not equality, not making sure everyone gets his or her "piece of the pie."

LL

If Limbaugh is a "new animal" in the media cosmos, he draws on some of the oldest strains in American thought, prairie populism blended with a dollop of common sense and a dash of xenophobia.

Steven V. Roberts, *U.S. News & World Report*

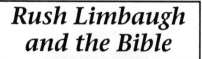

Rush Limbaugh and the Bible

6

The Poor You Have with You Always

*I*n the last week of His earthly ministry, Jesus told His disciples that He would not always be physically present with them but they would always have the poor (Matthew 26:11; Mark 14:7). There are always people in financial need.

These sentiments are echoed by Rush Limbaugh in "The 35 Undeniable Truths of Life," published in his newsletter. Truth 33: "There will always be poor people." Truth 34: "The fact that there will always be poor people is not the fault of the rich."[1]

Human society seems to always have poor people, but what can be done about them? How a person responds to the poor says quite a bit about him or her as a person. What is Rush Limbaugh's approach to the needy poor? Which social theories have helped to shape his attitude toward the poor? And how does his approach to the poor compare with Scripture?

The Deserving Poor

The Bible has some significant things to say about the poor—and also the wealthy. The general pattern throughout Scripture is that the deserving poor were to be cared for by those who had the means. The deserving poor were chiefly the orphans and widows of the community. Due to the social system of the day, widows and orphans were unable independently to care adequately for their financial needs. In the structure laid forth by God for the children of Israel, family or clan members were to care for their own needy. In the New Testament, the early church as well cared for its widows and orphans.

Instruction was given in the Old Testament for the care of the poor, whether a foreigner who was in need in Israel or an Israelite. These were not helpless widows or orphans but people whose poverty came about in other ways. Loans were to be made to the poor, but not at exorbitant interest rates. The poor should then be able to repay the loans and be debt free (Exodus

22:25; Deuteronomy 15:7–8). The way out of poverty was to work. Even though a jubilee was established by God to allow for the periodic wiping out of debts at 50-year intervals (Leviticus 25), in the intervening years the poor person was expected to work at paying off his debts.

While provision was made for granting loans to the poor so that they might plant their crops and feed their livestock, strong warnings were given about those who sought to avoid work. Various verses in Proverbs label the one who is lazy and refuses to work as a "sluggard." Two parallel passages end with the identical saying, "A little sleep, a little slumber, / a little folding of the hands to rest— / and poverty will come on you like a bandit / and scarcity like an armed man" (Proverbs 6:10–11; 24:33–34). In one passage, the author walked past "the field of the sluggard" and found it full of weeds and thorns, its walls fallen down. He took this object lesson to heart as a personal warning not to be like that person (24:30–32). In the other passage, the author urged the sluggard to get up from his sleep and go watch an ant storing food in order to learn industriousness (6:6–9). The deliberate avoidance of work had dire consequences, namely, poverty. The person who did not plow and plant seed would not have anything to harvest (20:4). Work was a necessary ingredient in a successful life.

In the New Testament, Paul warned believers to avoid idleness by following his example. He worked to pay his own way. He expected others to work, too. He established a firm rule: "If a man will not work, he shall not eat" (2 Thessalonians 3:10). Hearing of some who were idle, Paul urged them "to settle down and earn the bread they eat" (2 Thessalonians 3:12). If they refused they were to be shunned and made to feel ashamed, with the expectation that correction would take place.

Work Is Applauded

Just as the Scriptures condemn laziness, they applaud work. The order and rhythm of life was established by the pattern of God's creation of the world. God spent six days working to create the world and its inhabitants, but on the seventh day He rested. So He mandated that humans work six days but rest on the seventh (Deuteronomy 5:13–14). Built into the system is the Sabbath for re-creation and renewal.

The implication of the creation account is that, like their Creator, humans have been given creative ability. They were given the ability to work with their hands and they were placed in a setting where work would be necessary (Genesis 2:15). God assigned work to the first human couple. It was part of human self-identity from the beginning.

Proverbs says as much: "All hard work brings a profit" (14:23). Of Job it is said that God had "blessed the work of his hands" (Job 1:10). Paul told his followers, "Make it your ambition to . . . work with your hands, just as we told you, so that your daily life may win the respect of outsiders and so that you will not be dependent on anybody" (1 Thessalonians 4:11–12). Work brings self-respect, self-worth and a sense of usefulness. Work is not only important for supplying the daily needs of life, but also it has much to contribute to one's self-image. By working one is carrying out a divinely intended role. One is functioning within the purposes of the Divine economy.

The work ethic established in the Bible became the work ethic that has fueled the economic development of Western capitalistic countries. This is the thesis of Max Weber in *The Protestant Ethic and the Spirit of Capitalism* (1920).[2] Tracing the development of the Protestant ethic from the Calvinist side of the Reformation, Weber saw that Protestant countries were the capital-creating countries and that within mixed communities Protestants were the managers. Weber found that Calvinistic Protestants were the most highly productive people in Western Europe and America.

While some parts of Weber's work might be flawed, there is a core that remains solid. He has demonstrated that Protestantism has tended to treat all work as a "calling." Whether one was in a religious vocation or a secular vocation, work had a higher meaning beyond the mundane. Coupled with this, he has shown that Calvinism contained the notion that God blesses those who work. Financial success, according to Weber's thesis, resulted from an industriousness that was rooted in the Protestant propensity for hard work and frugality. These wealth-producing traits were part of a theological system which saw God as the rewarder of those who took seriously His call upon believers, whatever their work, to conduct their whole lives in light of His total daily care.

Democratic Capitalism

Another work on economic and social theory which helps to explain the way Limbaugh views the poor is Michael Novak's *The Spirit of Democratic Capitalism* (1982, 1991).[3] This defense of democratic capitalism and critique of socialism does not present capitalism as the perfect economic system, just the best one that humans have devised. As Novak looked back over the demise of state socialism in Eastern Europe, in his "Afterword for the 1991 Edition," he asserted his confidence in democratic capitalism: "My fundamental conviction has only been deepened by experience: no other system is as capable of raising the world's poor out of poverty." Discounting socialism as a failed dream and traditional agrarianism as bankrupt, Novak noted, "Meanwhile, the poor of the world, seeking opportunity, stream toward democratic capitalist lands. Thus the strongest moral claim for democratic capitalism is that it is the most practical hope for the world's poor: no magic wand, but the best hope."[4]

Novak sees democratic capitalism as deeply rooted in Christian theology. Crucial to capitalism is competition. Novak finds that Judaism and Christianity view life as a contest.[5]

Both Judaism and Christianity demonstrate that "God is not committed to equality of results. . . . Religious compassion does not entail leveling."[6]

This framework undergirds Rush Limbaugh's view of poverty and wealth. His emphasis is upon the individual. Just as in Scripture, he sees individuals as responsible for their lives before God, their ultimate judge. Thus, Limbaugh places strong weight on individual action. He firmly believes that individuals must take responsibility for what they make of their lives. They cannot expect Washington, or any governmental power center, to do for them what they must do for themselves. He calls on each individual to strive for excellence. The best opportunity for success, he feels, is having faith in oneself and making a definite effort to do the best he or she can to achieve excellence in every endeavor.[7]

Limbaugh would agree with Novak's argument: democratic capitalism provides the best opportunity for rich and poor alike. Since the start, America has fairly consistently provided the type of atmosphere where individual initiative is rewarded. Any attempt to remove competition, according to Limbaugh, is counterproductive. There must be a pursuit of excellence. One must be the best that one can be. While fairness and equality might sound like worthy ideals, they amount to leveling the field by lowering everyone to the status of those who do not want to try.[8]

Limbaugh's message ties in with Weber's

thesis that Calvinistic Protestantism, with its high regard for work and frugality, is supportive of capitalism. In Limbaugh's world people apparently get out of life what they put into it.

Are the Homeless Helpless?

Homelessness is one of the more visible manifestations of poverty. If someone is living on the street or in a park because he or she has no place to go, we naturally feel compassion toward the person. Here is someone with nowhere to go. He or she appears to be helpless. But Limbaugh questions the helplessness of many of the homeless. His solution to homelessness involves dealing with the root cause that brought people to the point of destitution, rather than creating permanent governmental bureaucracies to care for them. He might be called heartless by some, but over the long haul, maybe his solution is more compassionate.

Bringing people in off the street, only to make them permanent charity cases or creating an ongoing, underclass of poor people dependent upon government assistance is hardly humane.

No one wants to be dependent totally on the kindness of others with no hope of ever being able to care for himself or herself. Such an existence is personally demoralizing and destructive of self-worth. Would someone deliberately choose such dependency?

Some of the homeless, Limbaugh claims, choose to be homeless. They do not want to take on the responsibility to work and care for themselves.[9] These would fall into the biblical category of "sluggards," about which Proverbs warns. Others are homeless because they have drug or alcohol problems. These, he says, should be rehabilitated. Those homeless who are mentally ill, he adds, should be institutionalized. Those who are able to work should be shown the opportunities that are available and be given jobs. Limbaugh sees these as realistic steps to begin to solve the problem.[10]

What About the Rich?

We have established the fact that the poor will always be around, but what about the wealthy? As we have noted, one of Limbaugh's "undeniable truths" is that, while there will always be poor people, the wealthy are not to be blamed. For someone to have more, he would argue, does not mean that it comes at the expense of others. When there is recovery from a recession, someone will get rich. But he insists that to be rich is not a sin. Liberals might see the rich as sinners simply because they have money. They might want to rob the rich in order to equalize them with the poor. But Limbaugh maintains that achievers should not be punished merely because they are achievers.[11] Unfortunately, he notes, the successful are under assault. Those who have abided by the law and worked hard for what they own are now accused of stealing what they have.[12]

The question centers around material gain. Is wealth inherently evil? Biblical examples of wealthy people can be found. They are never condemned for their wealth alone, but they are judged for how they attained their wealth and for what they do with their wealth.

Isaiah warns those who benefit from oppressing the poor:

> *The LORD takes his place in court;*
>   *he rises to judge the people.*
> *The LORD enters into judgment*
>   *against the elders and leaders of his people:*
> *"It is you who have ruined my vineyard;*
>   *the plunder from the poor is in your houses.*
> *What do you mean by crushing my people*
>   *and grinding the faces of the poor?"*
>   *declares the Lord,*
>   *the LORD Almighty.*
>   (Isaiah 3:13–15)

Those who take advantage of the poor for their own gain stand to be judged harshly by God.

Jesus warned His followers, "Watch out! Be on your guard against all kinds of greed; a man's life does not consist in the abundance of his possessions" (Luke 12:15). He then told the parable of the rich fool, a person who lived totally for material gain, a man whose philosophy was "Take life easy; eat, drink and be merry." But God had words for him, "You fool! This very night your life will be demanded from you. Then who will get what you have prepared for yourself?" Jesus adds, "This is how it will be with anyone who stores up things for himself but is not rich toward God" (Luke 12:19–21). If wealth blocks spiritual growth and development, it is wrong.

Jesus Warned Against Riches

The danger of losing sight of spiritual matters in a material world is such a strong possibility that Jesus warns of it in several places. Just after the parable of the rich fool, in Luke 12, He tells His disciples to trust in God for their daily needs. "Life is more than food, and the body more than clothes" (12:23). God who clothes all of nature will take care of His children. He cautions them, "Do not set your heart on what you will eat or drink; do not worry about it. For the pagan world runs after all such things, and your Father knows that you need them. But seek his kingdom, and these things will be given to you as well" (12:29–31). The priority is clear: spiritual matters take precedence over material things. Jesus goes on to instruct His followers, "Sell your possessions and give to the poor. Provide purses for yourselves that will not wear out, a treasure in heaven that will not be exhausted, where no thief comes near and no moth destroys. For where your treasure is, there your heart will be also" (12:33–34).

Riches, material gain, possessions—can obscure the spiritual. We might not think that our possessions own us, but we all need to examine our attitude and our priorities. Toward what goal is most of our time and energy devoted? Is the spiritual—our relationship to God—really the most important thing to us?

Throughout Scripture God is depicted as being on the side of the poor and oppressed. Perhaps nowhere is this clearer than Jesus' reading of Isaiah and his application of it to Himself:

The Spirit of the Lord is on me,
  because he has anointed me
  to preach good news to the poor.
He has sent me to proclaim freedom for the
      prisoners
  and recovery of sight for the blind,
to release the oppressed,
  to proclaim the year of the Lord's favor.
      (Luke 4:18–19)

Judgment Day

When the day of judgment comes, our reward or punishment will be related to our treatment of the needy. Matthew records Jesus' words:

Then the King will say to those on his right, "Come, you who are blessed by my Father; take your inheritance, the kingdom prepared for you since the creation of the world. For I was hungry and you gave me something to eat, I was thirsty and you gave me something to drink, I was a stranger and you invited me in, I needed clothes and you clothed me, I was sick and you looked after me, I was in prison and you came to visit me."

Then the righteous will answer him, "Lord, when did we see you hungry and feed you, or thirsty and give you something to drink? When did we see you a stranger and invite you in, or needing clothes and clothe you? When did we see you sick or in prison and go to visit you?"

The King will reply, "I tell you the truth, whatever you did for one of the least of these brothers of mine, you did for me."

Then he will say to those on his left, "Depart from me, you who are cursed, into the eternal fire prepared for the devil and his angels. For I was hungry and you gave me nothing to eat, I was thirsty and you gave me nothing to drink, I was a stranger and you did not invite me in, I needed clothes and you did not clothe me, I was sick and in prison and you did not look after me."

They also will answer, "Lord, when did we see you hungry or thirsty or a stranger or needing clothes or sick or in prison, and did not help you?"

He will reply, "I tell you the truth, whatever you did not do for one of the least of these, you did not do for me."

Then they will go away to eternal punishment, but the righteous to eternal life.

(Matthew 25:34–46)

Our relationship to material possessions helps define who we are as persons. The Scriptures teach the priority of spiritual values over worldly goods. We are taught to work to supply our daily needs, but also that life does not end with the physical. Work is a noble endeavor, laziness leads to poverty and is condemned. We are instructed not to gain at the expense of others, yet we live in a competitive society. We must regulate our lives in such a way that we do not add to the oppression of the poor. The poor who are truly in need are worthy of charity to help to get them on their feet and headed toward self-support. Those needy poor who cannot fend for themselves must be provided for.

True compassion is to see that a lasting solution to a problem has been implemented. Limbaugh's criticism of a system that makes people dependent upon the government when they could and should be self-supporting is justified. On the other hand, he, along with us, should not blindly ignore the deserving poor who cannot help themselves. The poor will always be present. They should not be ignored.

---

[1]Rush Limbaugh, "The 35 Undeniable Truths of Life," *LL*, Vol. 1, No. 3, Dec. 1992, p. 10.

[2]Max Weber, *The Protestant Ethic and the Spirit of Capitalism*, trans. Talcott Parsons, (New York: Charles Scribner's Sons), 1958.

[3]Michael Novak, *The Spirit of Democratic Capitalism* (Lanham, MD: Madison Books, 1982), rev. 1991.

[4]Ibid., p. 421.

[5]Ibid., p. 344.

[6]Ibid., p. 345.

[7]Rush Limbaugh, "Let the Good Times Roll," *LL*, Vol. 1, No. 3, Dec. 1992, p. 12.

[8]*RLRS*, May 26, 1993.

[9]*RL*, p. 249.
[10]Ibid., p. 252.
[11]*RLRS*, June 17, 1993.
[12]*RLRS*, June 10, 1993.

Only a society that allows *individual* talents—gifts—to flourish will reap the benefits of human greatness.

LL

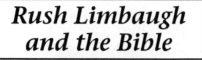

*Utopianism–
Stop Dreaming*

Mankind, it would seem, has always dreamed of better days. Days when peace and harmony would rule the earth instead of disharmony and war. Dreams of a utopian society have cropped up from time to time. Many of these have been confined to the mind of some thinker, others have been attempted in small scale communities. The one that has captured the most attention and has been worked for on the largest scale is what Rush Limbaugh labels

"Socialist Utopianism."[1] He sees it as the last gasp of socialism in the world today. He is utterly opposed to it in any of its manifestations and repeatedly attacks it in print and on the air.

Socialism grew out of the turbulent economic upheaval in the 18th and 19th centuries. As the Western world was becoming industrialized, quite a bit of displacement and disharmony arose. One response to this dislocation in world and national economies was an effort to eliminate competition through group ownership of the means of production. If production was held in common and controlled by the state, the argument went, class distinctions could be eradicated. All would receive what they needed to live on, in return for contributing their talents and skills for the common good. The extreme form of socialism is communism, where private property is abolished, at least in theory, and the individual becomes subservient to the common good.

The Fatal Flaw

The destruction of individualism, Limbaugh argues, is the fatal flaw in the socialist system. Socialism has always failed, and will always fail, because it offers no incentive to the individual. Only when individuals are free to own things for themselves and to work to better conditions for themselves and their families, can the creativity of humankind be experienced at its fullest. Limbaugh describes this core necessity for human individuality as "God-given." People receive their value from being seen as individuals before God and not some collective entity.[2]

Individualism is deeply grounded in the Bible. While individuals are seen as part of collectives and have certain duties in relation to the community, they stand before God alone. Each person is responsible for his or her own conduct.

The children of Israel were a community of God-followers, called out as a people, but individuals none the less. Believers in Jesus Christ are collectively known as the Church. There are duties incumbent upon group membership; reality, however, also dictates that before God the individual is the unit that bears ultimate identity. Each person is in God's image.

This individualistic view of human identity, while present in the Bible, is something more readily seen by people in the last few centuries than it was in earlier times. Communalism— belonging to the group—was the reigning perspective from Bible days until the time of the Renaissance and the Reformation. While the individual was always there, individual identity emerged with more force in the centuries after the Reformation. With the arrival of Enlightenment thinking in the 17th and 18th centuries, individual human development came to the forefront.

Since the Enlightenment, there has been increased tension between the role of the individual in relation to society. This tension, however, had always been there. What responsibility does the individual bear toward the community? Do individual desires and expectations preclude a concern for the common good? How might the common good be best served?

Socialist thinkers came to the conclusion that the common good would be best served if competition between individuals, classes, groups and nations could be totally eliminated. With the struggle to compete set aside, mankind could pull together and create a great new world. This utopianism, however, has had its head in the clouds. Socialism, when tried, has never worked out as intended. No matter how much leaders talked of the common good, of pulling together to benefit all, of setting aside petty individual concerns in order to establish a paradise for all, it has never happened. Pure socialism remains an illusion.

Why Socialism Fails

Why does socialism always fail? The individual stands in the way. Always there are private concerns that take precedence over the collective goals. Sometimes, as in the case of state leadership, totalitarian control and selfish special privilege usurp the intended goals of a classless sharing of goods. At other times the basic drive to better oneself conflicts with the "higher good" of living for the community. Whatever the level of society in question, when push comes to shove, there is an inner core of self that stands as the undeniable foil to socialist utopian schemes.

Living, as we do, in the post-Cold War reality

of failed Soviet communism, the collapse of Eastern European communism and the shakiness of world communism as a whole, we have an entirely fresh perspective. We are quite certain that this extreme form of socialistic utopianism is invalid. We look at socialism in the extreme and recoil. We want nothing to do with such a failed system. The long-rumored and well-documented horrors of the years lived under regimes more intent on self-preservation than meeting the needs of the people are exposed for all to see.

Where does that leave the more benign forms of socialism? After all, sharing and caring about our fellow human beings in a noncompetitive environment sounds like a noble venture.

Limbaugh, among others, has hit upon some of the central problems with socialism as he sees it functioning in America and the West. Finding socialism, in any form, utterly useless and detrimental to human well-being, he rejects the group he calls "Socialist Utopians."

How does he identify this group? What does he find objectionable in their program? First, he zeros in on their active anti-capitalism. They are linked by Limbaugh with the radicalism of the 1960s. Their agenda, he maintains, is to attack governmental and business institutions that support capitalism. They want to eliminate poverty by radically redistributing wealth in America.[3]

Limbaugh traces the core of this anti-capitalistic, socialist utopianism back to Franklin D. Roosevelt. According to him, Roosevelt began the process of making generations of people increasingly dependent upon the government for their existence.[4] By fostering dependence on government, socialism was instilled in the minds of the populace. The later generation of leftists have taken this government-dependency motif further. They see a utopia on the horizon as the economic productive power of America is harnessed to the cause of social betterment for all. They seek a planned society where those who have are taxed to support those who have not.

The Roots of Social Utopianism

The roots of this socialist utopian dream go back to the Social Gospel of the late-19th century. The Social Gospel thinkers held that if education could be improved, if industrial controls on the use of human labor could be instituted, if inadequate housing could be replaced by good—in short, if the human environment could be improved—society would see the kingdom of God on earth. Optimistically they predicted an era of peace with no competition, but only love and harmony.

Some of the Social Gospel agenda was adopted under Franklin Roosevelt's New Deal. In response to the dislocation of industrialization and the economic depression of the 1930s, the New Deal presented programs to alleviate the ill effects of America's changing society. Given the dire financial conditions, Roosevelt really had little choice but to try something. What he tried was a form of socialism. The government would step in to attempt to socially engineer the economy toward prosperity and to see to it that no one was left behind. In doing so, unfortunately, the creation of government dependency began. People dependent on the government to take care of them lose the incentive to do things for themselves. Why do, if the government will do for you?

This government-dependency has increased over time. Limbaugh charges that the basic philosophy of socialist utopianism is that big government is needed because the odds are against people thinking and working their way through life alone.[5] Dependency is fostered by those who are convinced that they can do for people what people left to their own devices cannot possibly do for themselves.

The result, Limbaugh argues, is an America where personal and national failure can be accepted. Excellence is set aside, replaced by an endless spiral of mediocrity. Average is about all that can be expected in such a situation.[6] Limbaugh firmly believes, however, in the power and ability of the individual to make a better life, despite current government attempts to level all. Self-reliance, not dependence on government, he contends, is the way to improve the lot of the poor and, at the same time, not hold back the rest of the people by steering the proceeds of their hard work into government hands.[7]

Limbaugh's criticism of socialist utopianism for being anti-capitalistic was to be expected. It goes against the grain of his individual-based, democratic capitalism.

Another central criticism of socialist utopianism that Limbaugh makes is in the area of its value system. He sees it as oriented around a moral relativism grounded in a secular humanistic approach, counter to Judeo-Christian traditional values. Self-gratification rules, he contends, because the traditional personal God of the Judeo-Christian tradition has been replaced by a vague, pantheistic concept of the god within everything. The basis of absolute morality has thereby been destroyed, leaving mankind on its own to dream about and seek an unattainable perfect society.[8]

What is the result of moral relativism? Limbaugh lays it out in an article in his newsletter entitled "The Left Was Wrong." Surveying the current declining moral condition of America, he blames the hedonism of the left. With the silent majority remaining silent and the dominant media of the nation captured by the forces of moral relativism, society has been in serious moral decline. Old values and established institutions have come under attack. If there are no moral absolutes, everything and anything goes. The results, he maintains, are devastating. Citing figures from former Secretary of Education, William Bennett, that show a shocking increase since 1960 in violent crimes, juvenile arrests, illegitimate births, one-parent homes and teen suicides, he singles out the lack of moral education as the chief culprit.[9]

Aroused from Silence

This critique of social utopianism highlights the conditions that have aroused some Bible-believing Christians from silence. The cultural war is on. How to turn things around becomes the key question. Certainly many such believers would want to align themselves with efforts to reinstitute moral education into our system. They would like to see people become less dependent upon government and more self-reliant. They see that the socialist utopianism of the left is headed in the wrong direction. We must not uncritically assume, however, that Limbaugh's brand of conservative democratic capitalism will usher in the kingdom of God.

Given the alternative, socialist utopianism, the choice for Limbaugh's side looks obvious. But when Christianity links up to any particular social, political or philosophical system, it must be aware that in endorsing that system, it has a tendency to "Christianize" the whole package. Is democratic capitalism the only system under which Christianity can thrive? Will evangelical and fundamentalist Christianity lose itself by mixing too intimately with a socio-political program, until it becomes a cultural religion and not the gospel of Christ? This is very real danger.

Whenever Christianity becomes too closely intertwined with the status quo, problems result. We must remember that the traditional Christian expectation of the kingdom of God involves an era of peace and prosperity under the direct rule of Christ Himself. Within evangelicalism and fundamentalism there is much discussion about when this kingdom of God will be ushered in and what it will entail. But we must never replace the biblical vision of the returned Christ's kingdom with visions of a man-made utopia, either from the left or from the right.

We may feel that Limbaugh's vision is better and more consistent with our moral outlook than socialist utopianism. But let us not work toward and expect an earthly kingdom to the detriment of the heavenly kingdom we await. The basic Christian mission is to change hearts, not to remake earthly society. Our message is personal salvation, not social salvation. While we support much of what we see and hear and can link arms in joint efforts with those who want to restore moral certitude to America, Christians have a higher agenda. If we lose sight of our true purpose—presenting the gospel of Christ to a fallen and doomed world—then we abandon our reason for existence. We cease to be different from the world around us. Our distinctives must be maintained.

---

[1] *RL*, p. 261.

[2] Rush Limbaugh, "Why Socialism Has Never Worked," *LL*, Vol. 2, No. 4, April 1993, p. 10.

[3] *RL*, pp. 261–264.

[4] *RLRS*, June 10, 1993.

[5] *RL*, p. 264.

[6]*RLRS*, June 8, 1993.

[7]*RL*, p. 263.

[8]Ibid., pp. 261–262.

[9]Rush Limbaugh, "The Left Was Wrong," *LL*, Vol. 3, No. 5, May 1993, pp. 1, 11.

Many of the women who have risen to leadership ranks in the movement are manhaters.

RL

A Man's Man

*T*he past 25 years have witnessed a virtual revolution in male-female relationships in America and the West. Rush Limbaugh, finding himself caught in changing and uncertain times, has reacted by reemphasizing traditional gender roles and attitudes. He has postured himself as a man's man, the defender of the way it ought to be. In the process he has said some things that have angered the feminist movement, often intentionally it would seem.

What are the traditional gender roles and attitudes that have been challenged? What are their roots?

Traditional Gender Roles

Traditional gender roles and attitudes in the West have their roots in the Judeo-Christian Scriptures. Female and male human beings were designed by the Creator, we are told in the Bible. This arrangement did not come about by accident or random chance. A purposeful Creator designed the species with two clearly different genders. From the beginning there have been gender distinctions, with differing roles for females and males. Since the beginning of recorded history each of the sexes has been working out the differing natures and roles of gender diversity. The design and intent was for the two sexes to unite in a bond for the procreation and preservation of human life. This very process would involve certain gender-related divisions of labor.

The Genesis account records that when Eve was presented to Adam, immediately after her creation by God out of man's rib, he knew that his search for a suitable helper was over.

> The man said, "This is now bone of my bones
>   and flesh of my flesh;
> she shall be called 'woman,'
>   for she was taken out of man."

> For this reason a man will leave his father and mother and be united to his wife, and they will

become one flesh.
(Genesis 2:23–24)

Man and woman were designed by their Creator to be together and to function together. Each would have a sphere of primary responsibility. Traditionally the male's role has been that of provider, while the female's role has been childbearer and nurturer. Before God, both were equal. In daily life, due to the nature of the division of labor built into the way each sex was designed, the female's role has been seen as subservient to the male. As the matron of the family her influence was great. But the actual legal power and status of women was restricted.

This essential equality of nature and yet inequality of roles is the pattern we find in Scripture. Paul notes that in the marriage relationship the wife is to be submissive to the husband (Ephesians 5:22–24). On the other hand, he declares that in Christ there is a oneness with neither male nor female (Galatians 3:28). The Genesis account of human beginnings records that both male and female bear the image of God (Genesis 1:27).

This essential equality of the sexes is too often overlooked. Both male and female of the species are special creatures in God's sight. Both stand before God as responsible creatures.

Limbaugh's Gender Views

Limbaugh describes this in more secularized language. He speaks of "nature" defining the roles of males and females. These roles, he states, are not easily changed because they are "ordained."[1] He claims that he has no difficulty with certain reasonable feminist goals, like equal pay for equal work.[2] So, he seems to agree to an essential equality before the law.

The attitude "That's just the way things are," permeates Limbaugh's discussion of the topic. He rejects the notion that we can ignore the differences between men and women, or that differences just do not exist, or that the differences are projected into the situation by men to keep women subjugated.[3] He leaves us with the feeling that certain things in life are "given," and no one can change them, so let's learn to make the best of the situation.

Men and women are not made the same. There are clear physical, mental and emotional differences in their make up. The emotional and mental differences between the sexes do not result simply from the socialization process of growing up. These differences are inherent within each gender.

Because there are inherent differences in the sexes, there will always be functions in life to which one of the sexes is better suited than the other. Not that there can never be any shifting of functions in times of necessity. Generally, however, the child nurturing role is best carried out by the female. God has especially equipped the female, not only physically, but mentally and emotionally, to nurture.

Limbaugh emphasizes this "natural" capacity

of women to care for child-rearing. He notes that society orients itself to make place for the child-rearing to be accomplished by the woman. Not that men are incapable of doing any child-rearing, but that the ideal is for women to have the major responsibility in the care of children.[4]

Human reproduction and the care of children have become the areas of greatest tension between the sexes in America. Women entering the work force have presented a challenge to the corporate structure, with attendant readjustments, many of which are still under way. However, it is the family structure that has undergone the greatest changes and challenges over the course of the last 30 or so years.

The Idealized Family

The idealized 1950s television family with Dad going off to work, the children going off to school and Mom staying at home, has evolved into two-income homes. Mother leaves the home for employment to add to the family income. Arguments are made as to whether this development was a necessity of the changed economic situation in the last half of the 20th century or a matter of families trying to get ahead of the pack. It is becoming more and more common for the whole family to go off during the day.

Some accommodations have necessarily been made in family scheduling and the division of labor in the home to adjust to this changed situation. Unfortunately, women often find themselves with more to do in the home before and after working hours than men, since child-rearing, as we have noted, has been their area of specialization.

The increasing divorce rate has created many single-parent homes, with the mother often left with the care of the children. This phenomenon, coupled with the increasing number of out-of-wedlock pregnancies, has presented major obstacles to maintaining the proper care and support of children.

Due to the fact that women bear the children and have primary child care duties during their children's early years, women of child-bearing years are at a distinct disadvantage in the job market. The uncertainty of when a woman might choose to start a family gives pause to employers in hiring and promotion practices. One might argue vehemently that it should not be a factor, but, nonetheless, it is.

Limbaugh makes note of the phenomena of women in the work force delaying childbirth until their mid-30s. Seeking to establish themselves career-wise before the onset of children, they then are faced with the biological necessity of choosing to have children then or never. Once children come women have to choose between staying at home to care for their children or returning to work. Limbaugh applauds those who have taken the time out of their careers to do the primary child care during their children's formative years, which he sees as essential to child development.[5] Bible believers would generally agree that ideally the mother should be caring for her children during the formative years.

Child-bearing and child care have become the central battleground in gender relations in America. What God has intended to unite man and woman—procreation and the sharing of children—all too often has been twisted by modern circumstances to be divisive.

The Feminists and Feminazis

Trying to gain some control over childbirth, the feminist movement has moved beyond birth control before the fact to birth control after the fact. It is this development that has caused Limbaugh to use the term "feminazi" to describe radical feminists who want to see as many abortions as possible. He does allow that this is a very small number of women. They, however, are influential feminist leaders. They see abortion as a powerful tool with which to fight male domination. It is a weapon to be used against men, without regard for the unborn children. It is a selfish act that cuts men out of the decision-making process.[6]

Behind the militant feminist movement, Limbaugh argues, is the notion that men are unnecessary and that anything that can be done to alienate women from men, should be done.[7] He accuses militant feminists of being anti-capitalism, anti-marriage, anti-family and anti-traditional values.[8] He is especially critical of the

National Organization for Women, the main feminist group in America. Quoting statistics that an estimated 30 to 40 percent of the membership of NOW is lesbian, he sees little wonder why the mainstream of American women are uneasy about being labeled feminists.[9]

Christians who believe the Bible would not accept the agenda of militant feminists. Their rejection of traditional family values, their support of abortion and lesbianism and their contempt for males place these women outside the parameters of supportable movements.

However, does rejection of militant/radical feminism mean that evangelical and fundamentalist Christians are anti-women? Does rejection of extreme views mean that the topic of women's rights must be abandoned? The Bible teaches equality before the Lord. The history of Christianity has provided opportunities for women to play a role in the Church and in society. Christianity has elevated women more than any other culture in history. Granted, at times women have been abused by actions taken in the name of Christianity and have been limited as to their public role in worship and leadership. However, the status of women in Western society has been steadily progressing, especially since the Reformation.

Opposition to the Equal Rights Amendment on the part of many Christians centers on a perceived fear of what it might mean for family cohesion. Anything that threatens the family and traditional values is suspect. Because God has ordained the institution of marriage and has put His blessing on the family, the long-established societal forces that are supportive of the maintenance of marriage and family need to be buttressed.

Ultimately a decision to stay home and care for young children or to reenter the work force is a personal decision made by each family. Does child-rearing preclude a career outside of the home for women? No, but the biblical view does mean that the priority should be the children. If a woman has been given the responsibility of children, there is no more important role that she can fulfill in life than raising them.

Sexual Tension

There is a certain amount of natural tension between the sexes. But open hostility is not what God had in mind. Women and men should treat each other with respect and should see each other as fellow creations of God. Men who put down women, men who abuse women, men who cavalierly impregnate women and abandon them are to be condemned.

Belittling statements and attitudes should be condemned as well. On this point Limbaugh is no angel. He defends the use of coarse language and off-color jokes around women. Especially at risk are women working in areas that are usually the domain of men. If women force admittance to formerly male-only areas, Limbaugh seems to feel they should expect gross behavior.[10]

But double entendre comments and questionable language should have no place in a Christian's discourse (see Ephesians 5:4). Limbaugh occasionally slips these into conversation both on radio and television, as well as in print. Limbaugh told one female TV caller that he was an old-fashioned guy, "from the waist up." Talking about a stop that President Clinton made in Hawaii, he slipped in a sexual innuendo concerning the large number of floral leis received by the president.[11]

In his newsletter section "Equal Time," he has included off-color material as well. Suggesting in "Rubber Revenues" that President Clinton might put a sin tax on condoms, he closed with a vulgar suggestion.[12] "Go-Go Girls," a piece on female urinals, was a somewhat crude note.[13] He seems to relish this risqué talk. On his television show, if the audience laughs at one of his off-color comments, he accuses them of having "dirty minds." After all, he is the paragon of virtue. He'd never stoop to such a level.

Limbaugh often deliberately puts women down, in the guise of attacking feminism. In discussing efforts to break down the barriers for women to be allowed into all-male military schools, Limbaugh disparaged feminists who wanted to be like men. He questioned their thought patterns, wondering "what it would be like to be an idiot for a day, or a woman for a day."[14] He may think he is targeting only feminists, but his scatter-shot blasts run the danger of hurting all women. In terminating his chapter on sexual harassment in *The Way*

Things Ought To Be, he apologized if anything he had written offended any women. But then he proceeded to close by expressing his love for the women's movement, "especially when viewed from behind."[15]

In an effort to defend the place of males in modern society, Rush Limbaugh comes off as quite a man's man. But men need not put women down in an effort to build themselves up. In God's eyes we are all "somebodies." Deliberately putting women down only serves to alienate the sexes.

---

[1]*RL*, p. 194.

[2]Ibid., p. 189.

[3]Ibid., p. 195.

[4]Ibid., p. 198.

[5]Ibid., p. 197.

[6]Ibid., p. 193.

[7]Ibid., p. 188.

[8]Ibid., p. 187.

[9]Ibid., p. 192.

[10]Ibid., p. 142.

[11]*RLRS*, July 12, 1993.

[12]Rush Limbaugh, "Rubber Revenue," *LL*, Vol. 2, No. 4, April 1993, p. 5.

[13]Rush Limbaugh, "Go-Go Girls," *LL*, Vol. 4, No. 6, June 1993, p. 5.

[14]*RLRS*, May 26, 1993.

[15]*RL*, p. 145.

We will never be able to recapture a lost life, never ever.

RLTS

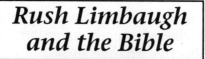

Rush Limbaugh and the Bible

9

The Cry of the Unborn

*R*ush Limbaugh is proud to be pro-life. He firmly holds the belief that human life begins at conception and he, except to save the mother's life, is opposed to abortion—the killing of that life. He links his opposition to abortion to upholding the very fabric of society. When human life is cheapened by allowing abortions, he argues, the door is opened further for crime, neglect of the elderly and the breakdown of the family. He maintains that "convenience" should not dictate who lives and who dies.[1]

Limbaugh bemoans the unfortunate attitude,

which has become widespread in America, that sex can be viewed merely as entertainment. He traces a collective change in attitude toward sex to the "free love" movement in the early 1960s, the beginning of the teaching of sex education in public schools and the attempted removal of absolutes from our national moral consciousness.[2]

Respect for human life is essential for a civilized society. However, a profound lack of respect for life has begun to taint our national moral framework. A major blow came, of course, in 1973 when the United States Supreme Court, in Roe v. Wade, legalized abortion in all phases of fetal development.

The Moral Breakdown

The universal legal availability of abortions in this country is seen by most Evangelicals and Fundamentalists as evidence of a moral breakdown. Legalized abortion has become symbolic of a lack of respect for the laws of life laid out in the Bible. When a human life can be terminated in the womb, largely for reasons of convenience, society has crossed a threshold. Most surveys conclude that very few abortions are done to save the life of the mother, because of health problems in the baby or because of rape or incest. Limbaugh cites a Planned Parenthood study showing 93 percent of abortions being done for social or birth control reasons.[3]

Various arguments can be advanced as to when human life actually begins. However, a human life begins to develop at conception.

This cannot be denied. Immediately upon fertilization, the egg begins to go through changes. Growth and development progress and nine months later the finished product emerges. This is one long, continuous process.

The design of the Creator was for the womb to be a safe place. This protected haven should afford each life a chance to grow, unhampered by disruption. To destroy and remove from the womb innocent human life is to circumvent God's intended plan. His designated goal is for life to live in and survive the womb. Unfortunately, accidents sometimes happen, or deliveries miscarry. But to deliberately destroy life in the womb is to play God, to usurp from the Creator the power of life and death.

Why do pro-life people get so upset about abortion? Because they see it as the taking of human life. In this they are opposed by those who label themselves "pro-choice" but who are, in reality, more pro-abortion than pro-choice. Limbaugh found himself in hot water with some listeners when he asserted that he was "pro-choice" with the hope that the choice was for life and not abortion. He objects to the term pro-choice because those who want to use that label do not actually favor choice. When someone is headed into an abortion clinic, he proposes, what is the harm if someone from Operation Rescue offers shelter, help with delivering the baby and adoption as an alternative? The problem is that abortion advocates do not want to offer a choice to women; they have an agenda. That agenda is to encourage abortion. Limbaugh depicts the pro-abortion forces in America as tied to two overwhelming impulses. First, a radical feminist movement sees abortion as power. They are the militant advocates Limbaugh labels "feminazis." Second, the large sums of money reaped by the abortion industry encourages its continuation.[4]

Thus, the question of whether or not to have an abortion is not open for discussion on either side of the issue. Those who form the extreme pro-choice element advocate abortion on demand and are pushing for as many abortions as possible. The pro-life or right-to-life movement is convinced that abortion is murder and is trying to stop as many abortions as possible. Any time there are two diametrically opposed groups advocating their views, there is bound to be confrontation. Limbaugh places the abortion dispute in the category of a potential "civil war."[5] That stage seems to have been reached already. Both sides are ready to do battle at a moment's notice.

A Woman's Right

Pro-choice advocates of abortion center their concern on a woman's right to do with her body what she wishes. If she wishes to abort a fetus, what is the harm? She should have the freedom to exercise this option if she chooses. It is an individual freedom issue, they argue. No one should be able to tell another person that she must carry a pregnancy to term. The flaw in the argument is that the decision was made after the fact, with a key player left unconsulted. The unborn baby has no voice. It has no rights. It is given no choice. Nor can it appeal to the courts. The choice is taken out of the hands of the one most impacted by the decision. Is that fair? Hardly.

Getting Rid of the Evidence

When sexual relations have transpired and a pregnancy has resulted, a moral choice has already been made. Life has begun, whether or not that was the intended result. Now, after the fact, people want to do something about the situation. The selfish decision is to disregard the life begun in the womb and merely get rid of the evidence.

Sexual relations have consequences. To enter into sex is to make a moral choice. One should be prepared to accept the responsibility for one's actions. But far too often responsibility does not enter the picture until a pregnancy is confirmed. Then the full weight of one's actions comes pressing in.

American society makes the choice to abort a child quite a bit easier by providing places to go where abortions are performed. Twenty years of legalized abortions have desensitized much of the public to the gravity of the act. Over a million and a half abortions take place every year. At least 30 million have taken place since Roe v. Wade in 1973. Everybody is doing it, but that does not make it right.

Morality cannot be a matter of democratic rule. We cannot just take a poll to see what should be right and what should be wrong. There are certain absolutes. That murder is wrong is one of them. If, indeed, human life does begin at conception, abortion is murder. In discussing when life begins, Limbaugh puts the matter to the test. If it is doubtful as to when life begins, he asks, isn't it better to err on the side of life and assume that life begins at conception?[6]

Robert Bork's View

However, he seems quite willing to put the whole matter of abortion to a democratic vote. He favors Robert Bork's view that since there is no basis for privacy rights permitting abortion in the United States Constitution, the state legislatures will have to decide the issue.[7] He seems quite confident that the American people do not want unlimited abortion and that is why pro-abortion forces fear a democratic resolution of the issue. While he gauges the country to be split down the middle on abortion, he told his radio audience that Americans want no federal funding of abortions. They want abortion legal, but not a lot of them. He applauded the reaffirmation of the Hyde Amendment banning federally funded abortions.[8] If abortion is recriminalized, he realizes that the problem will then be how to punish the offenders, since legalized abortions have been carried out for so long.[9] Even now, with physicians who perform abortions being criticized by pro-life groups, there is a decreasing number of them willing to continue performing abortions. This has resulted in radical feminists seeking ways to have "do-it-yourself" abortion methods ready.[10] It is probable that much confusion lies ahead before this issue will finally sort itself out.

Banning Abortions

Will the banning of abortions be effective even if laws against it are enacted? Probably not. The only real insurance against a woman having an abortion is to convince her that it is wrong. As Limbaugh told a caller, you have to change people's hearts by convincing them not to have abortions.[11] Ultimately, changing people's hearts is the answer. Short of that, laws making the availability of abortion services harder to obtain will give women longer to think about the grave step they are contemplating. Restrictions will slow the number of abortions, but not entirely stop them.

Some comment is needed about Limbaugh's infamous "caller abortions." His critics bring this long discontinued prank up as proof of his outrageousness. In an effort to prove the pain and reality of abortion, with the aid of a sound-effect vacuum cleaner noise, he extricated unwanted callers from his radio show. Over a two-week period he "aborted" around 20 callers. Upon discontinuing the practice, he told his audience that people seemed more upset at his offending callers and listeners than they were offended by real abortions. Caller abortions, which actually hurt no one, were objectionable. Violent, tragic actual abortions do not bother people because they are removed from the event.[12]

When reenacting caller abortions in his live stage shows, Limbaugh notices that some people become very uncomfortable. A few people even get up and leave the auditorium. He concludes that these must be people who have either had abortions or have paid for someone to have an abortion.[13] He seems to offer them no sympathy.

Christians who believe the Bible have something more to offer: forgiveness. In Christ Jesus there is healing of inner emotions through the grace and mercy of God. Our churches, pastors and support groups should be known as havens of mercy for those who come with broken lives. Repair and redemption are services we can offer. The church's love for the individual goes beyond anything the world has to give. May the Lord help us to reach out with open arms to these. May He also help us to reach out to those who need a viable alternative to abortion. May they find a place of safety, care and genuine concern with those who have experienced God's love, and are willing to share it with those in need.

---

[1] *RL*, pp. 50–51.

[2] *RLRS*, July 14, 1993.

[3] *RL*, p. 51.

[4]Ibid., pp. 54–55.

[5]Ibid., p. 50.

[6]Ibid., p. 56.

[7]Ibid.

[8]*RLRS*, July 1, 1993.

[9]*RLRS*, July 6, 1993.

[10]*RLRS*, June 21, 1993.

[11]*RLRS*, June 21, 1993.

[12]*RL*, pp. 62–65.

[13]Ibid., p. 66.

After the White House was swamped with calls protesting the admission of gays into the military, Limbaugh was singled out by the press as the leader of the lynch mob, even though he hadn't organized the phone-in. It didn't matter. Editorial pundits saw his sweaty palms all over this operation.

James Wolcott, *The New Yorker*

Limbaugh says there's a reason why certain views are minority-held views. Why should the gay community have special rights or be given preferential treatment just because it's a minority?

John McCollister, *The Saturday Evening Post*

The Gay '90s

*T*he increasingly relativistic moral atmosphere in America over the past several decades makes discussion of sexual orientation a somewhat threatening proposition. After all, in a day of "live and let live" and "anything goes" among consenting adults, to talk of taboos, of forbidden love or of unacceptable behavior sets one up as bigoted. At the risk of being called "homophobic," Rush Limbaugh has spoken out against the militant homosexual agenda which pushes for open homosexual preference and behavior in all areas of public life in America.

The unmistakable impression one gets from listening, watching and reading is that Limbaugh's main concern in the area of homosexuality centers on the disruption of the political and social fabric presented by open homosexuality. In fact, he speaks of a "political opposition" to the agenda of militant homosexuals but claims no bias against the lifestyle and is unconcerned with who is sharing a bed with whom.[1]

Gays in the Military

The controversy over gays in the military has brought the issue of gay rights to the forefront. Traditionally those who admit at the time of application that they are homosexual have been excluded from the American military. If a homosexual was inadvertently admitted to the armed forces and his sexual preference was later discovered, he was discharged from the service. Homosexuality was seen as incompatible with military service. Case closed.

President Bill Clinton, fulfilling a campaign promise to gay supporters, proposed a change. Initially he was pushing for full acceptance of gays and their lifestyle in the military. When this plan ran into opposition from key military and congressional leaders, he backed off to a compromise position. What was ultimately proposed was a policy paraphrased as "don't ask, don't tell, don't pursue." Inductees will not be asked if they are homosexual. However, once in the military, they are not to tell anyone that they are homosexual without its being presumed that they intend to engage in homosexual activity. Homosexual activity is forbidden by the military, and a person will be discharged for engaging in it. What is unacceptable then, according to this new policy, is homosexual *behavior*. Being a homosexual does not mean one cannot serve in the military. However, engaging in behavior identified as homosexual by military code, means discharge from the service. Homosexual activity, not merely being a homosexual, is deemed incompatible with military service.

This compromise, of course, angered militant gay rights activists. They expected full acceptance of their lifestyle. Their ultimate goal is for complete acceptance of homosexuality in all areas of American life. Positioning themselves as a persecuted minority, they are demanding that their lifestyle not be condemned or challenged by the majority.

Homosexual Rights?

Homosexuals depict themselves as victims who have suffered long enough for being different. They argue that homosexuality is an alternative lifestyle that should be tolerated in a free society without moral disapproval. They see nothing wrong with their way of life. None of their practices should bar them from full rights in the military or in society-at-large.

The change in policy on gays in the military upsets many within the military and outside of it who see this change as a dangerous first step toward open and active homosexual practices in the armed forces. Limbaugh, among others, predicts a flurry of litigation that will challenge the specifics of the policy, ultimately forcing changes that will open up more and more tolerance of homosexual practices in military ranks.[2]

Homosexual behavior that would disrupt the stability and affect the morale of the military is the crucial matter for Limbaugh, not private sexual orientation *per se*. He does not see a way to have gays in the military or in society without the expression of their sexual preference in some open way. Once homosexuality is openly exhibited, he predicts, there will be disruption and discord.[3] Maintaining the fighting ability of the military and the social cohesion within society seems to be Limbaugh's primary concern. Homosexuality is a divisive and disruptive factor; therefore, he wants to see it downplayed, if not eliminated.

The Biblical View

The Bible condemns homosexual acts, but not just because of their social effects. In fact, everywhere that homosexual acts are mentioned in the Bible they are condemned.

The infamous events at Sodom recorded in Genesis 19 involved attempted homosexual rape. The tragic account of a similar attempted assault in Gibeah (Judges 19) further points out the repugnance of homosexuality in God's sight. The Old Testament is very straightforward, "Do not lie with a man as one lies with a woman; that is detestable" (Leviticus 18:22). The punishment for such action is: "If a man lies with a man as one lies with a woman, both of them have done what is detestable. They must be put to death; their blood will be on their own heads" (Leviticus 20:13). This ancient law of Israel states clearly that homosexual activity is prohibited by God, under the harshest of penalties. Those who partake in such activity bring punishment upon themselves by their actions.

Homosexuality is a New Testament subject as well—together with lesbianism. Both are condemned within the context of the increasing waywardness of mankind, in blatant disobedience to God's direction:

> *Because of this, God gave them over to shameful lusts. Even their women exchanged natural relations for unnatural ones. In the same way the men also abandoned natural relations with women and were inflamed with lust for one another. Men committed indecent acts with other men, and received in themselves the due penalty for their perversion.*
> (Romans 1:26–27)

Among those who will not inherit the kingdom of God, according to Paul are "male prostitutes" and "homosexual offenders" (1 Corinthians 6:9). First Timothy 1:10 includes what some translations call "homosexuals" and the NIV calls "perverts" among those for whom the law was codified.

Gay Activity Forbidden

The message of the Bible is clear: homosexual activity is forbidden. To seek to reinterpret the Bible's pronouncements and accounts as not condemnatory of homosexuality, as some have tried, involves going against all the rules of biblical interpretation and leads to a debasing of the authority of God's Word.

Why is homosexuality condemned in Scripture? God has set forth a plan for mankind that is disrupted and defiled by homosexual activity. He has established the relationship of monogamous marriage as the sacred union of two individuals, male and female (Genesis 2:24; Mark 10:6–9). The design of God was intended to insure that a close, personal and fulfilling relationship would be possible. He specifically made men and women in such a way that, emotionally and physically, they both could enjoy, within a committed relationship, the deepest of unions. Homosexual behavior is a direct violation of God's design for humankind. The sexuality that God intended to be a positive, self-affirming and relationship-building force in life is perverted by same-sex sexual activity. What God purposed to be holy, is defiled. Those who defile are condemned.

What is the person with homosexual tendencies to do? Is homosexuality a choice? Is it genetically triggered or socially conditioned?

Can a person help it if he is homosexual, if she has lesbian tendencies?

The causes of homosexuality are complex. There seems to be some evidence from recent studies that there may be, in limited familial connections, a propensity toward homosexuality that can be traced to genetic causes.

Limbaugh doubts the validity of a study linking homosexuality to gene differences. If, after further study, it proves to be true, he predicts that large numbers of gays will switch from being pro-abortion to being pro-life. They will do so out of fear that parents will be able to check the genetic make-up of a child before birth, determine if there is a genetic propensity toward homosexuality and, if so, abort the child. He maintains that gays would probably be much more secure if homosexuality continues to be seen as a choice and not a gene-related aberration.[4]

Chastity the Only Sure Method

Whether there are genetic differences that push a person toward homosexuality, or whether it results from sexual abuse as a child or outright seduction by a homosexual, the response must be the same. Homosexual behavior is to be avoided. Just as there are other destructive urges in our fallen world that must be struggled against and conquered, often on a moment-by-moment basis, so also must homosexual behavior be resisted. However one came by the urge, it must be resisted. Chastity, abstinence, difficult though it may be, is the only sure way.

The avoidance of homosexual behavior is what the Bible urges and what society has traditionally mandated. Recent challenges to human and divine laws prohibiting homosexual behavior notwithstanding, it remains wrong.

Promiscuity within the homosexual community undeniably has facilitated the rapid spread of the AIDS virus. This disease has devastated the gay community. Promiscuity within the heterosexual community as well now threatens to spread AIDS throughout society.

Confronted with the specter of AIDS, many local school boards have resorted to condom distribution. Their intention is to protect their students against AIDS. The use of condoms, however, can never assure that the HIV virus will not be transmitted. Moreover, free condom distribution sends the wrong message to school-age young people. The adult community is saying to its children that sexual activity is all right, just as long as you try to protect yourself against disease and pregnancy.

Limbaugh courageously argues against condom distribution. He does not see it as a cure-all for the problem of sexual promiscuity. Calling free condom distribution "ridiculous and misguided," he argues instead for the teaching of abstinence. He repeatedly notes that, unlike condom use, abstinence works every time.[5]

Rush Is Right

Limbaugh is on the right track in urging

abstinence and in resisting the militant homosexual agenda. His "Condom Updates," which challenge the distributions of condoms, and his arguments against gays in the military are to be applauded.

Responding to the need of a group of concerned individuals who had organized a group to help children who were AIDS patients, Limbaugh faced rejection. He wanted to encourage his listeners to give money to this cause. He discovered that other AIDS groups had discouraged the foundation from accepting help from Limbaugh as they had earlier discouraged the use of a commercial made by former-President Reagan for the Pediatric AIDS foundation. Political persuasion apparently colors money when it is donated to fight AIDS, Limbaugh concluded.

Limbaugh has shown concern for some AIDS sufferers. In *The Way Things Ought To Be,* he chronicles the difficulties he had in donating monies to the Pediatric AIDS Foundation. He concluded that some money for AIDS research is more acceptable than other money. Evidently, he was stung by the rejection he faced and the rejection that former-President Ronald Reagan faced in trying to help this organization.[6]

Concern for homosexuals and for AIDS patients certainly should be a concern of the evangelical and fundamentalist community. While the Bible never excuses or condones an immoral lifestyle, the sinner is always extended love and shown the availability of forgiveness. Love certainly should be the attitude among churches and individuals if healing and restoration is to take place. Harshness and rejection will never bring people to Christ.

We can reach out to the homosexual with the gospel of Christ. This will not be easy. It has its pitfalls and dangers. But to do less would be to deny the very essence of the role of the Church in society. Will we offer a loving way out to the homosexual? Will we offer love and comfort to those dying of AIDS? Or will we stand accused by God and man as uncaring?

---

[1]*RL*, p. 84.

[2]*RLRS*, July 28, 1993.

[3]*RLRS*, June 23, 1993.

[4]*RLRS*, July 16, 1993.

[5]*RL*, pp. 130, 132.

[6]Ibid., Chapter 8.

. . . our culture has moved toward a new way of conducting business, especially its important business. The nature of its discourse is changing as the demarcation line between what is show business and what is not becomes harder to see with each passing day.

Neil Postman, *Amusing Ourselves to Death*

There is no escaping the connection between secular humanism and animal rights activism.

RL

"This World Is Not My Home, I'm Just a-Passin' Through"

*E*nvironmental extremists and animal rights activists come in for a good deal of criticism from Rush Limbaugh. Before we can judge from a biblical perspective the validity of his position on these two issues, we must understand the reasons for his opposition.

Limbaugh's fundamental opposition to environmentalists lies in the effect they have had or could have on the development of capitalism on this continent. He sees them as against private property. In seeking to take private land and make it public and protected, they are being hostile to the concept of private property.[1] He accuses "environmentalist wackos," as he labels them, of being eager to find fault with America and especially with its profit motive.[2] Much of the argument he has with environmentalists and animal rights activists comes from the dichotomy between his conservatism and their liberal political orientation.

Limbaugh believes that capitalism and the environment can peacefully share the earth. He claims we can still have a clean environment while we pursue prosperity. If we should damage the environment, we can repair it. Therefore, he advocates the continuation of industry and the maintenance of our American way of life.[3]

A Pro-Business Perspective

Thus Limbaugh's unconcern about environmental issues stems in large part from his pro-business political perspective. But it is deeper. He is optimistic about the earth's ability to renew itself. Maintaining that the earth is over 4 billion years old and that man has been here around 200,000 years, he asserts that man could not destroy the earth if he wanted to. His argument is that natural processes have been working in the environment for billions of years and yet the earth continues on its merry way.

Limbaugh cites ozone depletion as a case in

point. Volcanic eruptions have an adverse effect on the ozone layer. There have been eruptions for billions of years, yet the ozone remains relatively untouched. Therefore, Limbaugh concludes, whatever man does that might deplete the ozone layer is insignificant in comparison to nature's own processes. Any reduced levels of ozone are, according to him, only temporary. He dismisses those concerned about this issue as alarmists.[4]

In advancing his environmental arguments, Limbaugh discounts the "junk scientists" who do not do good science but have as their agenda the support of wild environmental crisis reports. He favors "more-reasoned" scientific evidence that coincides with his views.[5] He seems to pick and choose the reports he will believe purely on the basis of whether they go against or support his position.

Limbaugh's optimistic view of environmental issues stems in part from his belief that the world did not come about because of random events. It was planned. Limbaugh believes in creation.[6] One of his "undeniable truths" is that creation cannot be explained by the process of evolution.[7] He does not state which creationist chronology he supports, but he definitely does not hold to a young earth viewpoint, as we noted eariler.

Ultimately, Limbaugh admits, humankind cannot know everything. There are mysteries that cannot be understood by us. They must be accepted on faith.[8] This admission flies in the face of modern views of our ability to comprehend and control our world. As knowledge and technology have advanced in this century, humanist thinkers became confident that all of our problems and all of life's mysteries would fall to the advancing tide of science.

However, Limbaugh allows for mystery and faith to play a role in human life. He marvels at the precise placement of the earth that allows for life to flourish. He seems confident that our world did not result from chance.[9] He believes in God. We were created in God's image.

Furthermore, we alone were made in God's image. The "other animals" and all of nature are under our dominion.[10]

The Biblical View

Where does he get these ideas? They come from the Bible. Genesis 1:27–31 states:

> *So God created man in his own image, in the image of God he created him; male and female he created them.*
>
> *God blessed them and said to them, "Be fruitful and increase in number; fill the earth and subdue it. Rule over the fish of the sea and the birds of the air and over every living creature that moves on the ground."*
>
> *Then God said, "I give you every seed-bearing plant on the face of the whole earth and every tree that has fruit with seed in it. They will be yours for food. And to all the beasts of the earth and all the birds of the air and all the creatures that move on the ground—everything that has*

the breath of life in it—I give every green plant for food." And it was so.

God saw all that he had made, and it was very good. And there was evening, and there was morning—the sixth day.

David echoes the superiority of man.

You made him ruler over the works of your
        hands;
    you put everything under his feet:
all flocks and herds,
    and the beasts of the field,
the birds of the air,
    and the fish of the sea,
    all that swim the paths of the seas.
        (Psalm 8:6–8)

Our superiority as humans is tied to our creation by God in His own image. We are higher not because we have evolved to our present level but because we were created to be the primary rulers in God's world. We were given dominion over the animals and the right to use the plants of the earth for food. While we share this world with God's other creations, we alone have been created in God's image. We stand apart and distinct from all the others.

Limbaugh asserts that animals have no rights and can have no rights. They were not given rights by God nor can they, by some democratic process, be granted rights.[11] However, from God's statement in Genesis 1, it is clear that animals have been given plants for their food, just as have we humans. God has granted certain minimal rights to the animal kingdom. Limbaugh seems to agree with this when he allows that we have the obligation to treat animals humanely.[12] He also speaks of the responsible use of animals by humans so that no species are carelessly eliminated from existence.[13] Beyond this he seems unwilling to go.

Animal Rights

Limbaugh's main complaint is with radical environmentalists and animal rights activists who seek to place humans on the same level as animals. He objects to the notion that we are different only in degree from animals, not in kind. In opposition to this he argues for our uniqueness. He notes our creation in the image of God. But he then goes on to claim that this uniqueness, based on our ability for rational thought, can be maintained even if we believe in evolution and not in creation.[14] Here is where Christians must differ. When Limbaugh steps away from the truth of Scripture, he grants too much to the critics of creationism. He is on stronger ground when he reasserts the creation of man in God's image, part of which entails man's rational thinking ability.

Limbaugh seems most to want to explode the myth of the New Age concept that humans are one with the natural and animal world. This is the basis of many environmentalist arguments. He objects to the religious side of environmental extremism that is pantheistic, viewing the world as God and God as nothing more than the world. He accuses this group of holding back progress and wanting to reduce everyone to Third World conditions out of respect for nature.[15]

Evangelicals and Fundamentalists strongly support the view that the God of the Bible is not pantheistic. He is the transcendent God, different and distinct from the world He has created. He is the God who has expressed a personal interest in human beings. He has created humans to be higher than and distinct from the animals and from the rest of nature. It is this view of the created order that has helped the Judeo-Christian world to technological advancement.

At each step in the creation process God pronounced His created work good. Psalm 19 notes that the works of God declare His glory. Man and nature together were designed to display God's glory. But humans turned away from God into sin. Sin involved spiritual and physical consequences. Besides the spiritual separation that came between God and humankind, God put a curse upon nature. The ground was cursed with thorns and thistles; people had to struggle to feed themselves (Genesis 3:17–19).

The situation does not remain forever hopeless. The future redemption of believers entails a restoration of the formerly cursed creation. The Scriptures promise that "creation itself will be liberated from its bondage to decay and brought into the glorious freedom of the children of God" (Romans 8:21). Ultimately, as the effects of human sin are lifted from it, the entire created world shall once again fully reflect the glory of God.

Environmental Progress Expense

It must be admitted that some of the progress of our Western civilization has been at the expense of the environment. Nonrenewable resources have been exhausted. But are we headed toward a totally ruined physical world?

If we were to listen only to environmentalists, we would think we are on the edge of extinction. Limbaugh charges extremist environmental groups with using scare tactics to raise funds for their organizations.[16] On the other hand, there are legitimate environmental concerns, such as clean air and water, that must be addressed on a continuing basis.

There is an ongoing superintendence role which man performs in relation to the earth. This is a God-given duty. Genesis 2:15 states, "The LORD God took the man and put him in the Garden of Eden to work it and take care of it." Right from the outset man was given the job of taking care of the earth. The instruction was to preserve and care for the garden paradise. Subduing or having dominion does not mean that man can do with the earth as he pleases without consequence.

Between extremist environmental warnings and careless use of resources lies the middle ground of responsible management. We are to care for the earth. Adam's fall did not annul this command. Nor is it superfluous because authentic Christian believers know their true home is heaven. We are obligated to be good caretakers of this earth while we are here.

There is a danger in thinking that nothing mankind does can destroy the earth. Certainly nuclear weapons and nuclear waste, if mismanaged, present severe threats to our continued existence. We must be ever on guard against destroying or damaging even part of our earth.

---

[1] *RL*, p. 167.

[2] Ibid., p. 157.

[3] Ibid., p. 156.

[4] Ibid., pp. 154–155.

[5] Ibid., pp. 162–163.

[6] Ibid., p. 152.

[7] Rush Limbaugh, "The 35 Undeniable Truths of Life," *LL*, Vol. 1, No. 3, Dec. 1992, p. 10.

[8] *RL*, pp. 152–153.

[9] Ibid., p. 153.

[10] Ibid., p. 104.

[11] Ibid., pp. 102–103.

[12] Ibid., p.105.

[13] Ibid., p.106.

[14] Ibid., pp.104–105.

[15] Ibid., p.166.

[16] Ibid., pp.167–168.

A strong military militates against being attacked.

RL

12

War and Peace: Abroad and at Home

*W*e live in a fallen, imperfect world. This is a world in which force must sometimes be used in support of right. But it is also a world in which force is often used for evil. The defense of personal and national freedom often entails standing up to those who seek to bring harm.

War has been around for nearly as long as humankind. The Bible recounts a history in which God uses war to set up and to put down nations. He punishes some nations with military defeat, while He rewards others with land and booty taken in war.

Sinful humankind will find itself in periodic conflicts between peoples and nations until the end of time. Speaking of the last days, Jesus said, "When you hear of wars and revolutions, do not be frightened. These things must happen first, but the end will not come right away" (Luke 21:9). In fact, the Bible predicts a cataclysmic battle at Armageddon, in the Middle East, that will mean the end of human civilization on this earth as we know it (Revelation 16–19).

The authority of civil government mandates the defense of its people. In an imperfect world, such as ours, the only way that order can be kept between nations and among people within a country is through force or the threat of force.

The Necessity of Force

Rush Limbaugh advocates the necessity of force in maintaining our way of life in the world. Some of his "undeniable truths" present his views on war, peace and aggression:

- War is still an active option in a world governed by the use of force.
- Peace does not mean that there is no war or no nuclear weapons.
- Peace in a free country means that there are no threats.
- Peace cannot be reduced to understanding among persons.[1]

The general tone of these pronouncements is that war is a necessary evil. Even if nuclear weapons are eliminated, war will still exist. World peace appears to be unattainable for long. Talking to a point of understanding is not always successful; therefore, one must be militarily ready for war at all times. In his statement of beliefs at the beginning of *The Way Things Ought To Be*, Limbaugh asserts that peace between America and other countries depends directly on our military might.[2]

Limbaugh's praise of Ronald Reagan's toughness in dealing with the Soviet Union and other threats to our security is almost limitless. He saw Reagan as a strong leader, willing to rebuild our nation's military defenses at a rate that kept the Soviet Union off balance. Reagan talked tough. He called the Soviet Union an "Evil Empire." Tough talk coupled with a defensive build-up and plans for the Strategic Defense Initiative brought down the Soviet Union.[3]

Callers to his radio show accuse Limbaugh of being in love with war and killing. He maintains, however, that he hates and despises war, but those who seek to avoid war must have a strong defense so that attack from an enemy becomes unthinkable. The strongest deterrent to war, he asserts, is a strong defense.[4]

Military readiness, in the case of the Cold War between the United States and the Soviet Union, proved to be the deciding factor. Massive spending for the development of bigger and more powerful weapons on the part of the

Soviets was met through the Cold War years by resolve on the part of several United States administrations to be ready for all-out war if it came to that. Because nuclear war was something we prepared for earnestly, we avoided it. Thankfully, we have crossed into a less stressful time of reduced fear of all-out nuclear war. We can only pray it will last.

While the Cold War was going on, the United States engaged in armed conflict in various arenas around the world. These struggles were not unrelated to the standoff between the United States and the Soviet Union. The battlelines were drawn after the Second World War between the forces of democratic capitalism and the forces of world communism. This division of the world into two opposing camps has colored even our domestic politics.

Limbaugh has nothing but praise for the World War II era generation. He applauds their resolve, their determination and their patriotism. He accuses President Clinton and his fellow liberals of supposing the World War II generation "screwed up" by involving the United States in Vietnam. In contrast to President Clinton, who openly protested the war in Vietnam, Limbaugh maintains that he was never a war protester.[5] Indeed, he has supported all of America's wars, small and large, that have come in his lifetime.

Limbaugh has a problem with Americans who fail to back their nation's wars. One of his "undeniable truths" is that the movement for peace in America was pro-communist, either "by accident or design."[6] The traditional pacifistic religious denominations, who feel strongly that all war is wrong, and all those who opposed the war in Vietnam are painted, by Limbaugh, as being on the pro-communist side. His attitude: Any American who opposes anything America does is "dangerous."[7] He challenges the patriotism of anyone who questions whether America should use its military might overseas. Whether they are conscientious objectors to all war or question a particular American military action seems to make little difference to Limbaugh. To him, failure to support the United States is tantamount to siding with the enemy.

War sometimes cannot be avoided. Limbaugh refers to it as cruel and as the last option in relations between humans. The job of the military in war is to kill people and destroy things.[8] War is not a pretty picture. It never was and it never can be.

Women in Combat

Because war is an ugly business, Limbaugh sees it as no place for women. He opposes the introduction of women into combat roles in the military. Since women give birth they have the responsibility for the survival of the human race. Through the mothering and nurturing process they pass on civilizing values. He sees this role as too important to jeopardize on the battlefield. The thought of women being captured and tortured or coming home in body bags is something he is not sure the country would want to face. He is not, however, opposed to women serving in the military in non-combat areas.[9]

Just as relations between nations in our fallen world are contingent upon force or the threat of force, so also relations between individuals in sin-cursed human society are regulated by force or the threat of force.

God has instituted government to keep order. The Scriptures say:

> *Submit yourselves for the Lord's sake to every authority instituted among men: whether to the king, as the supreme authority, or to governors, who are sent by him to punish those who do wrong and to commend those who do right.*
> (1 Peter 2:13–14)

Government is supposed to punish wrong and reward good.

> *Rulers hold no terror for those who do right, but for those who do wrong. Do you want to be free from fear of the one in authority? Then do what is right and he will commend you. For he is God's servant to do you good. But if you do wrong, be afraid, for he does not bear the sword for nothing. He is God's servant, an agent of wrath to bring punishment on the wrongdoer.*
> (Romans 13:3–4)

Maintaining the Peace

Maintaining internal peace is the duty of

government along with caring for the national defense. In an imperfect world there will always be those who seek to do wrong and disrupt society. Internal peace is maintained through the use of laws. Laws are designed to protect the innocent and punish the guilty.

The way things are supposed to function and the way things actually work are sometimes not the same. We live in a nation of laws, but it is becoming a nation of far too many law-breakers. There seems to be a growing disrespect for law and law enforcement.

Limbaugh points to selfishness as the root cause of lawlessness. He finds that increasingly people want to do what they want to do without regard to how their actions impinge on others' lives or property.[10] If selfish, antisocial actions and even violent crimes are excused, he argues, then no one will be held personally responsible for his or her actions. This trend can only be arrested if children growing up are taught and adults reinforce the fact that laws do not oppress individuals, but rather laws create an orderly society. When all do their own thing, seeking pleasure, society cannot be orderly.[11]

Of course, lawlessness is nothing new. It goes back to the Garden of Eden and man's original rebellion against the law of God. Self and selfishness have always been man's problems.

Personal responsibility before the law is an issue that matters to Limbaugh. He criticizes liberal judges who see criminals as "victims of society," not fully responsible for their crimes because an inequitable society has driven them to behave in an unlawful manner. Such rationalizing of crime, he charges, allows the criminal to escape appropriate punishment.[12]

Arresting Trends

Personal responsibility and accountability are strongly taught in the Bible, as we saw earlier in Chapter 5. The opportunity to repent and seek forgiveness is available from God. Although God forgives, He does not necessarily excuse us from the consequences of our actions. As Limbaugh notes, our religions teach forgiveness, but we still must punish the guilty, otherwise society would degenerate into anarchy.[13] Limbaugh believes that criminals need to face the full weight of punishment under the law. He told a caller to his radio show that for too long we have not been serious and tough with the criminals in our country.[14] He wants more prisons. These prisons, he suggests, would serve to deter crime if they were places where criminals were worked, rather than allowed to enjoy all the luxuries that some prisons provide.[15]

It should come as no surprise that Limbaugh favors capital punishment. In response to critics who argue that the death penalty does not deter criminal behavior, he argues that we have to have "swift and certain justice," not the years of delay involved in most death penalty cases. Certainly then, we will be able to judge whether capital punishment is a deterrent to serious crime.[16]

The Death Penalty

The Bible contains far more laws that mandate the death penalty than any modern state has in its codes. Chief among the capital offenses is murder: "Whoever sheds the blood of man, / by man shall his blood be shed; / for in the image of God / has God made man" (Genesis 9:6). A partial list of capital offenses in the Bible includes: adultery (Leviticus 20:10); incest (20:11–12); bestiality (Exodus 22:19; Leviticus 20:15–16); sodomy (18:22; 20:13); witchcraft (Exodus 22:18).

Judeo-Christian civilization bases its system of laws upon principles that stretch all the way back to the beginnings of civilization. Those guilty of transgressing the law are to be punished. Support for the law is mandatory if society is to function in an orderly manner. This support for the law must include standing behind law enforcement officers who correctly do their job. It also means supporting the criminal justice system by seeing that criminals are appropriately punished for their offenses. In capital offense cases, where guilt has been established beyond any reasonable doubt, the death penalty is appropriate. Does this mean that the system is to function mercilessly, without compassion? No. But it does mean that justice must be upheld and order maintained.

Before Christ left His disciples, He asked them if they had swords (see Luke 22:36–38). He knew far better than anyone else that this is a fallen, not a perfect, world. Strife, envy, jealousy, contention and dispute mark human affairs. God has instituted government to protect citizens from outside aggressors and inside criminals. True peace will not be attained until Christ sets up His kingdom. Meanwhile, we must do what we can to maintain peace and insure justice on earth.

---

[1] Rush Limbaugh, "The 35 Undeniable Truths of Life," *LL*, Vol. 1, No. 3, Dec. 1992, p. 10.

[2] *RL*, p. 2.

[3] Ibid., pp. 231–234.

[4] Ibid., p. 183.

[5] *RLRS*, June 10, 1993.

[6] Rush Limbaugh, "The 35 Undeniable Truths of Life," *LL*, Vol. 1, No. 3, Dec. 1992, p. 10.

[7] Ibid.

[8] *RL*, p. 200.

[9] Ibid., pp. 200–201.

[10] Ibid., p. 173.

[11] Ibid., p. 174.

[12] Ibid., p. 170.

[13] Ibid., p. 171.

[14] *RLRS*, May 25, 1993.

[15] *RL*, p. 180.

[16] Ibid., p. 178.

Celeste, with connubial exasperation dripping from every word: "You're going to watch him *again*?"

"Well, yeah," I said, lighting up and punching in channel 13. "I said I'd write about him."

"But you've been watching him for a week, now," she said.

"Okay, look," I said, taking a long drag and deciding to come clean, "I can't help it: I get a *kick* out of Rush Limbaugh."

Frank McConnell, *Commonweal*

So multiculturalism, which portrays American history and even all of Western civilization as nothing but misery and racist, sexist, capitalist oppression, is the tool of revenge of many who have failed to assimilate and fit into the mainstream American life.

RL

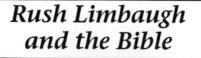

13

The White Man's Burden

When Rush Limbaugh defends the dominant culture as that which has made America what it is today, he is making a statement about all of the other cultures that are represented within our shores. He deflects criticism of the dominant culture by counterattacks on other cultures. He holds multiculturalism to be detrimental to America. He depicts those who advocate multiculturalism as villains.

Before we can discuss these issues, we need

again to lay out some background material.

The basic presupposition underlying Limbaugh's attitude toward American culture is that it is superior to the other cultures of the world. He asks: Why else would people flock here from the other countries of the world? Who else do the nations of the world turn to for technology? Where else do the peoples of the world turn in times of natural disasters or famines? America is, according to this line of thinking, the world's great hope.[1]

A Super Patriot?

Limbaugh declares flatly that America is the best country in the world and that he is tired of critics who want to alter history by making America out to be an "instrument of evil."[2]

There is a natural tendency for people to think that the country in which they live is the best country on earth. Perhaps this feeling has been heightened in America by our tremendous economic growth in our relatively short years of existence. Perhaps it is our preeminence as a military power or our leadership in world democracy that gives rise to these notions of superiority. In a sense they have been with us from the beginning.

Certainly Americans, since the early days of colonization, have thought of this country as a special place. The concept of the 17th century European settlers leaving corrupt lands to come to the pure, new land of freedom and opportunity has become part of our national consciousness. Those first settlers thought of America as a chance to start over and get it right. Under God's watchful eye and with His blessing, they would create a "city upon a hill" whose light of freedom would shine around the world.

The founding leaders of the new nation carried the idea that this country had a "manifest destiny," a special place in history. Our Declaration of Independence sounds the universal themes of freedom and opportunity for all. Here in this land of great natural resources democratic capitalism flourished and a great nation came into being.

Stepping back from the current situation, a person fairly asks, "What was it that made America great?" Limbaugh is a defender of Western culture. He sees America as the heir and perfecter of all that is best in the history of Western thought. He reacts angrily to those who want to replace the teaching of traditional Western culture with ideas gathered more broadly from different racial and gender perspectives. That is how he sees multiculturalists—as usurpers who want to change history and do away with the great ideas of Western culture, distorting the truth in the process.[3]

Multiculturalism and liberalism, in Limbaugh's view, go hand in hand. As he told his radio audience, the litmus test of liberalism is multiculturalism which creates hatred of America. Earlier in the show he pronounced multiculturalism the death knell of American culture because it attacked the central tenets of our heritage.[4] On the show the day before, he had charged leaders in the minority communities of the country with telling people of color that the way out of the ghetto is to get rid of white, heterosexual, male-dominated culture and replace it with multiculturalism.[5]

The point of multiculturalism, Limbaugh writes, is to discredit what this country stands for and to destroy our capitalistic way of life. Once this has been accomplished multiculturalists will replace the free enterprise system with socialism.[6]

But is this what multiculturalism is all about? Is it all just a trashing of dead, white, male Western cultural figures and their ideas? Is it an effort to completely revise history? Is it an effort to destroy capitalism and replace it with socialism? Or, rather, is it an effort to enrich our culture by examining and learning from other cultures? If the great works of Western thought are still studied alongside some of the influential works of other cultures, can this be bad? Granted an abandonment of learning about all the ideas that have made America what it is today would be a grave mistake. But is there any real harm and might we all not benefit from a study of different ethnic groups and women's contributions to our culture?

The clarion call of Limbaugh to all the peoples that make up the United States is to get a grasp of the central defining principle of American culture—self-reliance. People should be taught the things that will help them prosper.[7]

Multiculturalism's Economic Attack

At its base, Limbaugh's defense of the Western cultural tradition and attack on multiculturalism is economic. If people grow up without learning self-reliance, they will never contribute to society or their own well-being. He sees learning about other cultural traditions as counterproductive if the core American cultural heritage is not transmitted. He maintains that prosperity will come to an individual through access to the dominant culture, and access comes only through becoming a fully assimilated American.[8] As he told his radio audience, there is a chance for all in America if they will learn American culture and how to access America. He sees America as a land where "rugged individualism" and hard work pay off.[9]

Are multiculturalists really asking that the dominant culture be ignored in favor of ethnic studies? If so, then indeed they are doing a disservice to their students. Survival in our society depends on being able to negotiate in the language and system of thought of the majority culture. Failure to learn how to function in society will be detrimental to individuals and communities.

While there has been one dominant culture that shaped and continues to shape this nation, many other cultures have contributed to the richness that is America. Must these other cultures be slighted in order to boost "Americanism?"

The "melting pot" theory of immigrant absorption has largely been supplanted by the notion that ethnic identity remains an important shaper of individual and community identity. A stew pot, if you will. The "melting pot" never entirely blended differences. The waves of immigration at the end of the 19th century and the early years of the 20th century tended to form ethnic settlements in geographic areas, both within cities and across the countryside. Many of these areas still exist. Festivals displaying national dress, dance, food and customs are a yearly feature in these communities. If anything, the newer waves of immigration have not proved to be any less susceptible to the blending in and the losing of their ethnic and cultural identity than the earlier waves. Western Europeans, of course, have assimilated more completely than most because American culture is largely Western European in orientation. The degree of variance of a group from the dominant culture seems to slow down the blending-in process.

What each wave of immigration faced was the need to learn enough about the dominant American culture to be able to function and get ahead. Often immigrant parents pushed their children to "be Americans" so that they could advance in society. If language and customs needed to be abandoned or trimmed to "make it" in America, then so be it. But what the first and second generation immigrants discarded as unimportant in America, the third generation has attempted to recover. It is this period of recovery of ethnic roots that we find ourselves living through now.

Room for Everybody

America, the land of freedom, should supply enough room for all ethnic groups to recover or maintain a sense of ethnic and cultural identity, without the dominant culture feeling threatened. Perhaps it is the fear of being overwhelmed by immigrants that has prompted the current opposition to multiculturalism. We have seen this fear before in our history. The massive immigration at the end of the 19th century gave rise to the restrictions placed on immigration in the 1920s.

Whenever supporters of the dominant culture feel sufficiently threatened, they will react. Sometimes they overreact. It is true that those of other cultural backgrounds must adapt to the dominant culture if those groups are to successfully participate in American society. But does that preclude the study of other cultures in our schools?

Rush Limbaugh argues that the maintenance of ethnic cultural heritage belongs in the homes, religious institutions and neighborhoods, not in the public schools. He feels that our cohesion as a nation is fragile and that multicultural studies will weaken public education and our national identity. Pointing out cultural variety will foster ethnic tension and division.[10]

Limbaugh continues to hold the view that America is a melting pot where the racial

167

division can be overcome if we do not dwell on our cultural differences. He wants everyone to behave as Americans, support American culture and, thereby, blend into a harmonious whole.[11] While this is a noble goal, it overlooks the tenacity of ethnicity and the reality of racial diversity in this country. Some allowance must be made for ethnic and gender differences in our school curriculum.

Can we learn from other cultures? Yes, indeed. We have as our heritage a noble set of values. We feel that these values have made our country and our way of life the best on earth. These values have led to economic prosperity. But that does not mean that selected other values from other traditions might not benefit and improve our way of life. To cut ourselves off from the world of ideas because they are not part of Western tradition is shortsighted.

Thriving on Variety?

The grand idea of one American people, while a magnificent concept, has not worked out that well in practice. *Should* Americans blend into a single homogeneous culture, or do we thrive on variety? Are we a nationality, or many different peoples living together under universal ideals? One monolithic culture does permeate American society. But our sense of freedom should allow people to be themselves, ethnically and culturally, while at the same time being Americans. The dominant culture, its language, history, manners and customs must be taught in our public schools, but an exposure to and respect for other cultures should not be out of place there.

Bible-believing American Christians should be at the forefront of such integration. They hold that in Christ, within the community of believers, there should be no distinction of nationality. "There is neither Jew nor Greek, slave nor free, male nor female, for you are all one in Christ Jesus" (Galatians 3:28). Jesus' instruction was to "go and make disciples of all nations" (Matthew 28:19). As Christianity has spread throughout the world, it has taken on various flavors and styles of worship. As long as the core beliefs are strongly emphasized and biblical doctrine is firmly adhered to, allowance can be made for various cultural expressions. The day of making "cookie-cutter" Western Christians out of Third World converts has passed.

Missionary outreach has exposed churches and individuals to the multiplicity of cultures within the community of believers. It is obvious that God loves and welcomes all peoples into His kingdom. Revelation 7:9 indicates that all peoples will be represented before the throne of God in heaven. This should sensitize us to accept people of all cultures and to learn about their ways of life. Of course, should they come to live in America, they will have to learn our ways, just as we must learn their ways if we go to live in their cultures. We can, however, learn to appreciate other styles and customs without feeling threatened.

[1] *RL,* p. 213.
[2] Ibid., p. 45.
[3] Ibid., p. 204.
[4] *RLRS,* July 13, 1993.
[5] *RLRS,* July 12, 1993.
[6] *RL,* p. 212.
[7] Ibid., pp. 206–207.
[8] Ibid., p. 205.
[9] *RLRS,* July 12, 1993.
[10] *RL,* p. 213.
[11] Ibid., p. 206.

Does he really believe in everything he says? Of course not. This is radio, and Rush is a performer. . . . He takes special delight in people not knowing when the act ends and the real Rush begins.

Michael Arkush, *Rush!*

I am delighted to be the country's guiding light
through the confusion, tumult and chaos.

LL

Prey on or Pray for Those in Authority?

*R*ush Limbaugh dislikes the political policies of President Clinton and liberal politicians, and he takes every opportunity to let his audience know so. If a policy is seen by Limbaugh to be faulty, he is quick to point it out. Part of the freedom we have to voice opinions on politics in America involves dissent. Disagreement with public policy and working within the system to seek to change policy is an important right and duty in this country.

I urge, then, first of all, that requests, prayers, intercession and thanksgiving be made for everyone—for kings and all those in authority, that we may live peaceful and quiet lives in all godliness and holiness.
(1 Timothy 2:1–2)

The Bible is clear, however, that we should have an attitude of respect for elected leaders.

Respect for Authority

Respect for authority is one of the basic elements on which society operates. Saint Paul calls for respect and honor for governmental authorities.

This is also why you pay taxes, for the authorities are God's servants, who give their full time to governing. Give everyone what you owe him: If you owe taxes, pay taxes; if revenue, then revenue; if respect, then respect; if honor, then honor.
(Romans 13:6–7)

He indicates that governing authorities rule because God ordains government. Those who do right have nothing to fear; those who do wrong should justly fear punishment (see 13:3–4).

While criticism of someone's position on an issue is a welcome part of the public discourse that makes our participatory government function, personal attacks are something else. Muckraking and personal attacks have a history in

American politics dating back to the 19th century. Recent years have seen an acceleration of personal attacks in our election process. This increase has alarmed some observers of the political process. Apparently it has also turned off some voters.

How does one express legitimate criticism of a person's views in a constructive way? He or she can do this only by sticking to the issues, making policies the focus and not the person.

Although Limbaugh is an entertainer and a comedian, he also wants to be taken seriously as a political commentator. Why else would he publish a book and newsletter and sponsor the National Conservative Forum? He enjoys appearing on political analysis-type television programs. He seems to be seeking a certain level of respect within not only the world of media and entertainment but in political circles as well.

The tremendous popularity of his radio and television shows indicates that he is getting his message across to an increasingly large audience. People are responding, one can assume, not just to how he presents what he has to say, but to what he says. Callers applaud his forthrightness in speaking out and note that he is not afraid to take on the "big boys" of the political world.

Limbaugh and Clinton

When President Clinton was elected to office, some thought Limbaugh's television and radio shows would drop in the ratings. With the election campaign over, they expected his audience to lose interest in politics. Such has not been the case. President Clinton has become Limbaugh's number one topic, providing a target for all of his anti-liberal sentiments. Every indication is that Limbaugh's popularity has grown since the '92 elections.

It must be remembered that President Clinton was elected by a plurality, not a majority. More people did not vote for him than voted for him. Limbaugh taps this potential audience. His conservative listeners and other disaffected voters tune in to hear what he is going to say about the latest presidential decision—or indecision.

Early in Clinton's presidency, Limbaugh began the process, on both radio and television, of counting the number of days of the administration so far, and how many are left. He assumes Clinton will be a one-term president. He announces that America is being "held hostage" and that the country is being subjected to "The Raw Deal" of Clinton and the Democrats. His television show has often begun with a cartoonish depiction of a scene outside the White House. Early in Clinton's term the White House photo was doctored so that it had a peace symbol and hippies hanging around smoking pot, or Clinton's head with shoulder-length hair superimposed on it. One opening scene showed a sunrise and had a photo of Clinton crowing like a rooster. Certainly this moves beyond criticism of a person's views to open ridicule and disrespect.

Rush Limbaugh's technique of playing a bit of

a person's speech or press conference remarks, stopping the tape and offering his commentary, works effectively as a tool to shoot holes in a person's position. But it usually is not fair to the speaker, especially if the remarks are taken out of context, which is often the case. Worse yet, Limbaugh will often laugh at what has been said, or he will mimic the person's voice, mannerisms or style. For example, he repeatedly makes fun of the way Tennessee's Senator James Sasser says the word "deficit." He often repeats it several times and chuckles. Is this fair? No. Does it show respect for an elected official? No. Does it get a laugh? Sadly, yes.

How Limbaugh presents his criticism of government leaders should matter to earnest Christian believers. We are given clear instruction that we are to respect those in authority over us. If, indeed, God has ordained that there be civil government with authority to rule—and He has—then respect for that authority is essential. When someone shows disrespect for a mayor, governor, congressperson or president, how should we react? When Limbaugh holds a government official up to ridicule, should we laugh and say "Sic 'em, Rush!"? We cannot say we value respect for authority if, at the same time, we go along with or revel in someone's open ridicule of public officials.

Declining respect for authority is a problem in modern society. As supporters of the God-given authority of civil government, can we afford to cheapen that authority in any way? When we endorse ridicule of governmental figures, we are only adding to the problem.

In the Scriptures we are told:

> *Remind the people to be subject to rulers and authorities, to be obedient, to be ready to do whatever is good, to slander no one, to be peaceable and considerate, and to show true humility toward all men.*
> (Titus 3:1–2)

What does it mean to be subject to rulers and authorities in a democratic society? It means to work within the system to bring about changes. What does it mean to be considerate and show humility toward all men? It means to have respect for people, especially government officials, it means to deal with the issues and not personalities. Does this passage of Scripture and the admonition in Romans 13:1 to submit to authority eliminate any disagreement with our governmental leaders? No, but we are to obey and respect authority.

Limbaugh seems to want it both ways. As *TIME* magazine said of him, "He wants to be taken seriously as a pundit by those he convinces and indulged as a comedian by those he might outrage."[1] As a conservative he advocates respect for authority, but when he ridicules elected officials he undercuts that very authority. He feels it is his right to have a little fun. He, after all, is only joking. Can't liberals take a joke? He does not seem to want to take responsibility for the impact his style of deprecatory humor has upon his audience. But it clearly lowers respect for individual elected authorities, especially Democrats, and most especially those he sees as liberals.

If Limbaugh would stick to the issues and not cross the line into personalities, he would be on much safer ground. Since he *does* engage in personal attacks upon elected officials, those who believe in God-ordained governmental authority need seriously to question whether they should support this type of humor and ridicule.

---

[1]Richard Corliss, "Conservative Provocateur or Big Blowhard?" *TIME*, October 26, 1992, p. 78.

But man is a spiritual being. If his faith in God is destroyed, the void will be filled with something else.

RL

Rush Limbaugh: Politically Incorrect, Biblically Correct?

*R*ush Limbaugh is judged as politically incorrect by the prevailing mood of the intellectual community. Political correctness is a recently coined term to describe a situation that has developed on many college and university campuses across America. Political correctness asserts that the old standards of what is good and bad in literature, philosophy, art, morals, were set by a restrictive, European-centered, male-oriented system and must now be challenged. To be politically correct, an individual must hold to the view that truth is relative. Nothing should be judged as "better" than any other thing. There are no absolutes.

Political correctness demands tolerance of all points of view. The surety of a statement cannot be assumed simply because civilization handed down a time-tested, well thought out position. The politically correct will ask, who came up with this idea? What perspective does it represent? What motives stand behind its formulation? Whose place does it enhance?

Taken to its extreme, there can be no absolute standards of right and wrong, good or bad in a politically correct world. Cultures are relative, as are all the elements within a given culture. Equality becomes the watchword in a politically correct framework. Everything should be treated equally, objectively and without bias, since everything has the same relative value.

The use of the term *politically correct* has spread. One hears it applied to people and statements outside of higher education all the time.

Defender of Tradition

Limbaugh is a very vocal defender of tradition. He feels that the standards of American society must be upheld because they are under attack by forces that will demoralize the nation and lead it into anarchy. Because he feels this threat so intensely, he lashes out against any and all people or forces he judges to be feeding the other side. Many of his statements challenge the "politically correct" assumptions which underlie the causes he targets. Therefore, by today's standards, he would definitely have to be categorized as politically *in*correct.

When Limbaugh speaks in support of absolute moral values based upon Divine law, he may be politically incorrect, but he is biblically correct. The politically correct would disagree. They would say that there are no moral absolutes, everything is relative. Besides, these laws and the Divine authority held to be behind the laws are the product of one culture among many. It is judgmental to place one set of moral values higher than other sets of values derived from different conditions.

Criminals Are Responsible

Arguing that criminals are responsible for the crimes they commit may make Limbaugh politically incorrect, but he is biblically correct. That individuals are responsibile for their actions is part of the Bible's message. Political correctness seeks to excuse criminals for unlawful behavior because of their upbringing, poor environment or other contributing factors.

Speaking out against abortion may not be politically correct, but it is biblically correct. The Bible supports the sanctity of human life.

Condemning homosexual behavior and opposing the admission of gays to the military is not politically correct. The Bible, however, always condemns homosexual activity.

Considering human life superior to animal life may not be politically correct. But the Bible teaches that man has been given dominion over the earth and its animals. As beings created in the image of God we humans are distinctively set above all of animal creation, no matter what our physical similarities to animals.

Innate Differences

Believing that there are innate differences between males and females that define certain roles in life is not politically correct. However, the Bible holds that males and females have different roles—roles that make each distinct.

On a number of key points, Rush Limbaugh is politically incorrect but biblically correct. There are other issues, however, where the lines are not so clear. His condemnation of pacifists is too broad. Just because one is opposed to a war in which the United States becomes involved does not mean that he or she is anti-American. There are good people who as a matter of conscience object to all wars. The church denominations that traditionally have stood against all war should not be lumped with those who oppose a particular war for less noble reasons.

Limbaugh's view that we cannot really destroy our environment overlooks not only the negative effects of nuclear waste and clear-cut forest land but also the positive biblical injunction by God to us to be earth's caretakers. The attitude toward the environment espoused by Limbaugh will lead to callousness and arrogance toward the world we are to superintend. Rather than caretakers we become unwise stewards of the world God has created and placed us in. We are superior to the animal world, but we are to treat animals humanely.

Although the Bible speaks unequivocally in support of work and industry, there are deserving poor for whom we must care. The Bible clearly teaches that those who have the means should care for the deserving poor, lending money to help them get back on their feet. Limbaugh comes across as indifferent toward the poor, as if all of them want only to be taken care of by the government. This overlooks the dislocation we are going through now, and which economies go through periodically, in which the levels of production can leave some people out of work for long periods of time. There are also the poor who, through disability or similar hardship, cannot care for their needs. The Christian gospel teaches greater compassion than Limbaugh seems willing to allow.

Support for Traditional Values

Christianity, as a major element of traditional American culture, generally benefits when older established ways are reemphasized. It cannot be denied that Rush Limbaugh speaks out regularly in support of some of the traditional values which Bible-believing Christians also support. As a vocal spokesman for traditional values he is gaining some attention for important issues.

The problem is in the way he raises these issues and the attitudes he may foster.

Rush Limbaugh prides himself in being an entertainer. He has proven that he can draw an audience in print, radio, television and personal appearances. He uses comedy adeptly. His clever production devices are highly entertaining. Incontrovertibly, he is a master showman.

But although Limbaugh views himself as primarily an entertainer, he wants to be taken seriously, as we have seen. And there is tension. Delete the humor and Limbaugh would not have as large an audience. Delete the seriousness, and he would be without a cause. Either way, his impact would be diminished.

Some of Limbaugh's humor is off-color, and not just in the minds of the listener, where he would want to fix the blame. He uses language, on occasion, that must be condemned as vulgar. Making fun of feminists, advocates for the homeless, environmentalists and others spills over to hurt well-meaning people, whether intentionally or not. By exaggerating the extremes of liberalism and then painting with the same brush any who even mildly endorse the position, he is unfair to moderates. This seems to be an intentional tactic.

Part of the problem is the public persona of Rush Limbaugh. He deliberately heralds himself as the defender of all that is good in America. He sees himself as the lone advocate of truth against the distorting forces of the dominant media. He seems to suggest to his audiences that they will not find truth except in his words. He is on the cutting edge; everyone else is off the mark. Repeatedly he tells his audience they have only to listen to him; he will tell them the truth.

It is the truth Limbaugh says he is after. But is it the whole truth? Not really, for no one is objective, everyone has an agenda. Although he told his radio audience that they only think he is on a crusade to destroy liberalism, that he really has no carefully plotted effort, that he merely gets up every day and answers the phone, it is not that way.[1] While he wants to be seen as an entertainer, which he is, he must be seen as far more than merely a funny fellow who says some witty things. He is more than just a guy on the radio who talks to people on the phone. He dispenses conservative political views. In fact he is the leading dispenser of conservatism currently on the American scene. His "getting at the truth" is getting at his particular brand of the truth. It is a selective choice of certain issues. If scoring means exaggerating his opponents' views to the point of distortion, he feels justified. Apparently the end justifies the means.

Paragon of Virtue

Rush Limbaugh depicts himself in his public persona as the paragon of virtue, an excellent example to America's youth. He asserts himself as someone we can trust with our children. He claims he would be the ideal mate for America's daughters, if mothers had the option to choose. His radio announcer introduces him as not just a man but "a way of life." He calls our day "the era of Limbaugh." He once bragged to his radio audience that he is a visionary, able to see all political possibilities.[2] On another occasion he told them they shouldn't want anything else if they have him and his show.[3] His assertion is that the talent he has is "on loan" from God, that he makes almost no mistakes and that it takes only half his brain to defeat liberal arguments. These and other claims may be dismissed as entertainment bravado, mere showmanship. However, he has created the intentional impression that when he is before the camera or the radio microphone he is on a special mission.

In jest or reality, no one seems to know, he has created the image of a proud, arrogant, self-righteous man who is entrusted to single-handedly save the nation from the clutches of evil.

Ego vs. Message

Deliberate or in fun, Limbaugh's ego gets in the way of his message. *He* becomes the focus.

Limbaugh boldly asserted to his radio audience that "everything" in life was about money.[4] Another time he stated that all people do what they do for the money, even if they won't admit it.[5] No one would deny that the profit motive propels the economy of the world. There are, however, plenty of people who do things without money in mind. This broad assertion on the importance of money discounts the many servants of Christ who selflessly commit their lives to His service. Dedicated people who seek to serve God do so without thought for the money involved. The history of the church is filled with examples of those who gave up all to follow Christ. Not everyone is controlled by money.

Christians who seek to live under the authority of Scripture must be careful about endorsing Rush Limbaugh and everything he says. His attitude is not one of love and helpfulness but of confrontation and condemnation. He often puts people down in harsh, unkind ways. He does not usually show proper respect for those in authority. He is not always fair in dealing with the issues.

Imitators

Imitators are springing up nationally and locally. Randall Terry has a national show; others have regional followings. The radio waves are filled with talk shows that take in listener calls. Television has its share of talk shows, too. As Limbaugh notes, many copycats are coming along, but he doubts that they will be able to say the same things in the same way.

When asked if he plans to run for political office, Limbaugh flatly says he will never be a candidate for anything.[6] He says that acquiring an audience and attracting voters are two different things. Media people, he notes, usually do not fare well in elections.[7] Despite these protestations, it remains to be seen whether he has political aspirations.

Should Bible-believing Christians listen to and

watch Rush Limbaugh? Each of us must decide individually. Should we get our entire picture of the world through his eyes? We should read, view and listen widely, always with a finger on what the Scriptures have to say. Will we find Limbaugh's views always consistent with the Bible? Not always, as we have noted, though many are. Certainly we should not imitate his cavalier attitude toward people and his lack of respect for those who govern.

Just as Limbaugh discounts a socialist utopia, those who expect a capitalist utopia will be disappointed. A perfect social order awaits the return of Jesus Christ to set up His kingdom. Meanwhile, we Christians should be cautioned against attaching our Christian faith too closely to any person, any political party or any agenda. We are to be the Church. Our mission is always beyond specific political parties or ideological movements or personalities. Our focus must be on changed hearts through the redeeming power of the gospel of Jesus Christ. If we lose sight of this, we have lost our way.

---

[1]*RLRS*, June 10, 1993.

[2]*RLRS*, June 9, 1993.

[3]*RLRS*, May 24, 1993.

[4]*RLRS*, June 8, 1993.

[5]*RLRS*, June 18, 1993.

[6]*RLRS*, June 22, 1993.

[7]*RLRS*, July 7, 1993.